HELP,
I'm Retiring!

By Rick Parkes

Contents

Acknowledgments

I would like to express my gratitude to the many people who saw me through this project and to all those who provided support to me through the many coffee-shop conversations and brainstorming sessions that ultimately helped me shape my observations and opinions for this book.

I appreciate the many individuals who allowed me to quote their remarks and assisted me in the editing, proofreading, and design of this publication.

I would especially like to thank my copy editors, Tom Bowen and Lars Dolder, for helping me focus my prose and get the book from my mind into print and ready for publishing.

I would be remiss if I did not mention Anjanette Mitchell and Lea Webb and the fine work they did in assisting me with this project.

Nikki, my daughter, and my son, Sean, are both very creative people, and it goes without saying that I love them both. Nikki is an interior designer and Sean is a sound engineer and musician. In part, it was their creative spirit that spurred me on in my quest to produce a must-read book for anyone in retirement or anyone approaching that unique stage of their lives. My endeavor was to provide some surefire planning to enable retirees to not outlive their money, and it is my sincere hope that this book accomplishes this. Above all I wish to express my eternal gratitude to my wife, Dianne, whose patience during this journey was inexhaustible and whose contribution to this project was invaluable. Our forty-nine-year-marriage has been a wonderful experience for me, and this is largely due to her unfailing support. She knows that I love her, but it seems appropriate to say that out loud here. She also recognizes my second love is that of helping families achieve their life goals. I will always be grateful for the support and encouragement my family gave me in this endeavor in spite of the time it took away from them. Last and not least, I beg forgiveness of all those who have been with me over the course of the years and whose names I have failed to mention here.

The Parkes Family

Preface

Is it me, or is everybody these days passing out investment advice?

I was logging on to the Internet the other day, and I was utterly amazed at the proliferation of blogs, articles, and websites devoted to finance. If the World Wide Web is truly an information superhighway, there has to be a traffic jam at the intersection of Investment and Advice.

Walk into your local bookstore and you will find thousands of books on personal finance. The magazine section has an entire rack devoted to the category. Keeping up with it all has gone from exhausting to impossible.

Television now has several channels dedicated to money management. It is almost comical to watch the talking heads dueling like knights of old, each willing to opine ad infinitum on the subject of how you should handle your finances. As soon as one of these "experts" finishes uttering a strong opinion, his colleague begins the counterpoint.

At the office, unsolicited investment advice is as ubiquitous as post-it notes and paper clips. Even our neighbors can be counted upon to share with us their latest and most astonishing stock-market secrets.

Yet all we want to do is build and preserve a retirement nest egg...one that will allow us a measure of independence and carefree living for our sunset years. But we are left scratching our heads, overwhelmed, and wondering whom to believe.

So, in this book, I attempt to cut through the fog with the searchlight of simplicity and hopefully focus that luminous beam on what people really want to know:

- How can I make sure that my money outlives me?
- How can I retire in reasonable comfort?
- How can I know that my retirement fund will keep up with inflation and taxes?

And just because these are important questions doesn't mean that the answers have to be complicated.

But like all things worth doing, becoming investment savvy requires some perseverance and study. Throughout this book, I intend to deliver some straight talk about not only why you should think about your money and your future, but also how you should go about it. I also intend to pull back the curtain, as it were, and let you see the entire picture for yourself, enabling you to make decisions rooted in facts, research, and common sense instead of in hopes, wishes, and unsound theories.

Chapter ONE

It's Okay To Trust Yourself

It is just as possible to receive bad financial advice as it is to receive bad medical advice. A wise doctor once reminded me, "It's your body. You live in it, not me." I gave that a lot of thought. He was right, of course. I may not have medical training, but I know when something hurts far better than the doctor does.

The same is true when it comes to handling your money. It's your money.

If the advice you are given doesn't fit you, don't be afraid to say no. If it isn't clear to you, don't hesitate to stand up, hold your hand out like a traffic cop, and say, "Hold it. I don't understand that!"

Let's say you walk into a store to buy a pair of shoes, and for some odd reason, the salesperson tries to convince you that you should buy a pair that is one size too small. You squeeze your feet into the shoes, but your toes hurt. You can barely stand up in them, much less walk. Would you buy those shoes? Of course not. Why? Because they're your feet. And you know what size you are comfortable with.

It's the same with investment advice. If a recommendation doesn't fit you, don't be afraid to shake your head "no" and just walk away from it.

But if you feel that it does fit you and your personal circumstances, and it comes to you from a reputable source with a fiduciary responsibility to you (in other words, not from someone merely seeking profit for himself/herself), then consider acting on the advice in the same way that you would act on the advice of any other professional, such as an attorney or a doctor.

But it is wise to always ask yourself, "If I implement this decision, how will I feel about this decision ten minutes from now, ten days from now, or ten years from now?" If the answer to that question is "good," then it's okay to say "yes." But only do so after gathering all the information you need to make that determination. When it comes to your money, an uninformed decision is nearly always a bad one.

Why The Sudden Interest In Retirement?

Earlier I mentioned the seemingly endless stream of information coming out about investments and retirement. Why the sudden information explosion? There are two reasons:

Reason 1—Baby boomers are approaching retirement.

Baby boomers are those folks who were born between 1946 and 1964 when there was a steep increase in the birthrate in America after World War II. Statistically, baby boomers are the largest generation in the history of America, numbering around 77 million, and—who would have thought it—they are nearing retirement.

Boomers are responsible for over half of all consumer spending. They buy 61 percent of all over-the-counter medications, for example. Not surprisingly, they account for about 88 percent of all leisure travel.

It has been estimated that a baby boomer turns fifty every 7.5 seconds in America. Obviously, these "golden boomers" are going to impact all areas of American life in retirement.

Evolution of Life Expectancy

- Year 1970 - average life expectancy was 70
- Year 1980 - average life expectancy was 73
- Year 1990 - average life expectancy was 75
- Year 2000 - average life expectancy was 76
- Year 2010 - average life expectancy was 78
- Year 2020 - average life expectancy was 78 (the year we like to forget)

People are living longer, medical science is better and people are taking better care of themselves.

https://www.macrotrends.net/countries/USA/united-states/life-expectancy

Reason 2—Americans are living longer.

At the turn of the century in 1900, the average life expectancy in the United States was forty-seven. In 1970 it was seventy. In 1980 it was seventy-three. In 2000 the average life expectancy was seventy-six. In

2010 it was seventy-eight and in 2020, it was seventy-eight.

So, the good news is we are *living longer*. The bad news is we are *living longer*. Here's what I mean.

For the first time in history, there are now more seniors than there are teenagers. Workers are retiring earlier, either voluntarily or otherwise. If you are one of those baby boomers, it is probable that your parents and grandparents either died while still working or died shortly after retiring. But many of your generation will live twenty to thirty years after they finish working.

So, what do we do with this information? This is great news if we make financial plans to accommodate our longevity. It is not so good news if our quality of life is diminished because we outlive our resources, lose our independence, and become a burden on our family.

What if, in our senior years, our health fails? What then?

One of the myths of the animal kingdom is that the ostrich, when sensing danger, will bury its head in the sand to hide from the threat. It's not true, of course. It's an optical illusion. These large, flightless birds aren't sticking their heads in the sand. They are merely using their beaks to dig holes, either looking for food or preparing a nest for their eggs.

But humans exemplify this mythical behavior when they fail to acknowledge the facts about growing older and experiencing failing health.

FACT—In 70 percent of all couples age sixty-five or older, one of them is in a nursing home.

FACT—The average stay in a nursing home is about 835 days or 2.29 years.
FACT—The average cost of a nursing home stay is around $89,000 - $100,000 per year.

How do we take care of these needs? Certainly not by ignoring them! Even if we are fortunate enough to avoid a nursing home stay and the medical expense that accompanies it, living longer is likely to erode our resources as inflation eats away at the value of our savings.

The Government Isn't Going To Take Care Of Us. Sorry.

I wish it were otherwise, but the government is not going to take care of us in our sunset years. Even if we fix the much-discussed problem of the Social Security system having too many beneficiaries and too few workers to support it, that still won't solve the real problem. Social Security is simply not enough to take care of us. But that really shouldn't come as a shock. Social Security was never *intended* to be enough. It was intended to be a financial side dish, not the main course. You won't be happy with what's on your plate in retirement if Uncle Sam is the only cook you're counting on for your vittles.

Don't Count On Your Employer Either.

For the last few years, company pensions have been steadily replaced by plans like 401(k) and 403(b). This shifts the burden of savings and investing from employers to employees. These plans can be confusing, but they also can provide us with lots of opportunities. It's up to us to make our plans for the future. The good news in this regard is that it really is possible to do just that.

Chapter TWO

Beware Of The Inflation Demon

Many of you reading this book may be old enough to remember the late 1970s and early 1980s when Jimmy Carter was in the White House. The mini skirt was in vogue and men wore flashy polyester leisure suits with flare-bottom trousers. It was also a time of double-digit inflation, which made both interest rates and prices jump through the roof. CD rates climbed to above 15 percent. Was that a good time for investors? No!

What? You mean 15 percent isn't a good return on money? Not really, if your account was being eaten up with higher taxes and roaring inflation. The bottom line was that, when figuring in taxes and inflation, your account was in negative territory when all was said and done. It was the most illusionary of financial times. Even though you received higher rates of return on paper, the real purchasing power of your money did not keep pace.

Sure, you got a pay raise of 10 percent, but living expenses were up 15 percent! Your CD at the bank may have returned 15 percent interest, but with surging inflation your real rate of return was below zero. Fixed investments were, as they say, "under water" and "in the tank."

As I'm writing this book, inflation rates are relatively tame. The inflation demon has been chastened and put back in his cage—for now. He's still around, and who knows when he may rear his ugly head again to threaten our financial foundation?

Could It Happen Again?

Because of the shape of its coastline, the state of North Carolina is said to have its "chin" stuck out, waiting for and taunting the windy fist of each hurricane that comes near. The years 1954 and 1955 were two of the most active hurricane periods ever recorded in the Tar Heel state. Hurricanes Hazel, Carol, and Edna devastated miles of pristine coastline and destroyed thousands of homes that had been built on the beach. You would think that the destruction caused by those three sinister sisters would have served as a deterrent to building so close to the ocean. But not so. The 1960s saw the beginning of one of the largest coastal building booms ever. Within ten short years, the beaches that had been so devastated saw their populations triple. The lessons of the mid-fifties seemed forgotten—until the1990s, that is, when the next wave of hurricanes hit.

When it comes to managing money, prudent investors recognize the inevitable reality of cycles and prepare for them. If we have learned anything about the past, economically speaking, it is this: history repeats itself, and things have a tendency to run in cycles. Could the days of double-digit inflation return? Of course they could. But the sudden erosion caused by unexpected, violent economic storms is nothing compared to the steady pounding of what we might term "reasonable" inflation. An inflation rate of 3 percent is considered to be reasonable. We have come to expect it. But when you crunch the numbers, you will see that, at that rate, the purchasing power of your dollar is cut in half in roughly twenty-three years. That means that in two decades you will need twice as much money as you do now to buy what you are buying now. Prudent investors learn to look for the net return in several ways, which we discuss in subsequent chapters of this book.

Chapter THREE

Be Wise With Your Social Security

If you spoke with a financial professional about 20 years ago, you were probably introduced to something called the "three-legged stool of retirement." The best stools consist of three legs; add a fourth and you can introduce wobble, cut it down to two legs and you don't have a self-standing stool at all. Back then, when investment was a simpler undertaking, many advisors preached that a well-rounded retirement plan likewise consisted of three essential "legs." The ideal retirement plan, so they said, included a pension, Social Security, and personal savings. Beautifully simple.

As you can imagine, the illustration hasn't held up to the test of time. While some may be fortunate enough to retire with a pension, most soon-to-be retirees these days are not. And for the few privileged to get a pension, it's likely a whittled away version of what our parents retired with.

With pensions going by the wayside, the "three-legged stool of retirement" is but a pitiful two-legged stool. And now, a second of its legs may be under attack—Social Security.

Social Security's History

The year was 1935. The United States was in crisis. The Great Depression was in full swing with almost 80 percent of the country out of work. To make things worse, a war was brewing across the sea. Germany was stripping Jews of their civil rights and intensifying their persecution each day while Italy invaded Ethiopia. It would only be a matter of time before the American military had to intercede. But how? The American people were struggling and downtrodden. It probably won't surprise you to learn that Alcoholics Anonymous was introduced in 1935. Or that the Parker Brothers' game "Monopoly"—where players could pretend to achieve wealth and power—became an instant success.

In Washington D.C., President Franklin D. Roosevelt was furious. For years, every attempted solution had failed to improve the nation's economy. It was enough; Roosevelt was taking matters into his own hands. He was determined to make a lasting change, to boost the American people's morale and infuse the country with hope. Thus, Roosevelt's "New Deal" was born.

The New Deal included a number of programs, projects, and reforms to stimulate the economy and to launch a new post-depression era in the United States. One facet of the New Deal was what President Roosevelt dubbed the "Social Security Act." It was designed to ensure lasting financial stability for a generation who had nothing in the way of retirement savings.

On August 14, 1935, President Roosevelt signed the act into effect. He announced to a crowd of onlookers and press representatives: "[Social Security] represents a which is being built, but is by no means completed—a structure intended to lessen the force of possible future depressions, to act as a protection to future administrations of the government against the necessity of going deeply into debt to furnish relief to the needy—a law to flatten out the peaks and valleys of deflation and of inflation—in other words, a law that will take care of human needs and at the same time provide for the United States an economic structure of vastly greater soundness.

For many decades, Social Security accomplished that objective. But eventually, things started to go wrong. Social Security faced a serious funding issue. When Roosevelt introduced Social Security in 1935, he chose 65 as the magic number for retirement—the age at which Americans first qualified to draw from Social Security. These days, most Americans live to see age 65 and to deduct their share from the Social Security pot. In 1935, however, it was a different story. The average life expectancy for men was under 60. Women typically made it to 63. Either way, the average American never lived to see a Social Security check. The few that did live past 65 hardly placed a financial burden on the United States government. By the 1980s, Americans were already living much longer than people had just 45 years earlier. More qualified for Social Security than Roosevelt could ever have imagined. How would the country's leaders address the mounting strain on Social Security's reserves? With taxes, of course.

In 1983, Ronald Regan became the first president to tax Social Security. Under his Social Security Amendment, up to 50 percent of Social Security was subject to taxation as part of regular provisional income if your base annual income was $25,000 as a single person or $32,000 for couples filing jointly.

That wasn't the end of it, though. In 1993, President Clinton again reformed the Social Security system. He introduced a law which allowed for 85 percent of one's

Social Security benefits to be taxed. Single beneficiaries would have to earn over $34,000 and couples more than $44,000.

But here's the kicker—the income thresholds that qualify people for taxation on their Social Security benefits have not increased in the nearly 30 years since Clinton's reform. Social Security benefits and average income, on the other hand, have both increased substantially. That means that almost every American family, if they don't plan in advance to avoid it, will be taxed on their Social Security.

If you're surprised to learn that your future Social Security benefit is *probably* subject to taxation, you're not alone. Many find out only when their accountant informs them at the end of the year. Social Security is not a straightforward income. You and your neighbor could both get a check for $30,000 from the Social Security administration, but how much of that sum each of you gets to keep could vary widely. It all depends on your other income sources and how much you make from them. So, how can you determine exactly what income triggers Social Security taxes? Is it possible to avoid those taxes altogether without subverting the law? Let's find out.

Reportable Income

Whether your Social Security is taxable or not depends on how the Internal Revenue Service categorizes your other income. It can be reportable or non-reportable. That isn't to say that I'm suggesting you neglect to report income to the IRS. I'm afraid that would be illegal. So, what am I talking about?

The IRS, for whatever reason, has decided that some income sources contribute to provisional income and therefore form the basis for your taxes. That income is called reportable. Everything else is non-reportable. The following are some of the most common reportable income sources:

Certificates Of Deposit. Most soon-to-be retirees have a substantial amount of money stored at a bank and often that money is invested in certificates of deposit (CDs). It's one of the most popular "safe" investment options. CDs are not subject to stock market variation which does indeed put them at the low-risk end of the investment spectrum. The bank pays interest on CDs, but most choose to let that interest roll back and add to the CDs total investment. But how does the IRS view that interest? Even if the money never leaves the bank and never passes through your hands, it is still reported as income on your tax return. Besides how annoying that is unto itself, it can also contribute to total income that can trigger taxes on your Social Security.

Mutual Funds, Index Funds, SMAs. Just like with CDs, the interest earned on bond funds—even if immediately reinvested—counts toward your reportable income. If you have a mutual fund, you probably choose to use the end-of-year distribution to buy more shares. It may even happen automatically without your conscious involvement. That can make it a rude surprise when it shows up on your tax return. Again, we have a case of money that never passes through your hands contributing to your taxable income and potentially setting off Social Security tax. Money like the interest on CDs and mutual fund distributions falls into a category that I call "phantom income." You may never see it; it easily slides under the radar. But when tax season rolls around you can feel the effects of phantom income in a big way.

Dividends. It is easy for dividends to impact what you pay in Social Security taxes. Dividends have many positives. For example, they can be taxed at a lower rate if they are "qualified" dividends. But still, they add to your reportable income and can thus contribute to your having to pay taxes on Social Security.

Step 1: Provisional Income	$30,000 in Social Security benefits (1/2=$15,000) + $45,000 in IRA withdrawals = $60,000 of provisional income
Step 2: First Threshold	$60,000 of provisional income - $32,000 (first threshold for married filing jointly) = $28,000 above first threshold x .5 = $14,000 of taxable benefits
Step 3: Second Threshold	$60,000 of provisional income -$44,000 (second threshold for married filing jointly) = $16,000 x .35 = $5,600 of taxable benefits
Step 4: Calculate	$14,000 +5,600 = $19,600
Step 5: Check the Max	.85 x $30,000 (total Social Security benefit) = $25,500 Compare your results in Step 4 and Step 5. Whichever is lower is your taxable amount.

Municipal Bond Interest. Municipal bonds attract many investors because they are income tax free and can sometimes be exempt from state taxes. But don't be fooled. Interest from municipal bonds may still be included for tax purposes as part of your provisional income and can thus set off taxes on your Social Security.

IRA Distributions. I saved this one for last. When most people unnecessarily qualify themselves for taxes on their Social Security, it often has to do with their IRA distributions. Almost all retirees these days depend on distributions from their IRAs to supplement retirement income. That money was stashed away years ago as tax deferred. Now when it's time to withdraw, Uncle Sam wants his share. Often, however, it doesn't end with taxes paid on IRA distributions. That money also counts toward reportable income which can set off taxes on Social Security, further chipping away at your retirement nest egg.

Non-Reportable Income

So, what's non-reportable? The IRS uses your adjusted gross income (AGI) to calculate how much of your Social Security, if any, should be taxed. AGI is your total gross income minus exemptions and deductions. To calculate how much of your Social Security is taxed, the IRS adds up your AGI, one-half of your combined Social Security benefits, and any tax-exempt interest you receive. That includes all your dividends and all your tax-free municipal bond interest. It also accounts for pension income, IRA distributions, earned income, and so on. This total is called your *combined income.*

If your combined income exceeds the limits provided by law, your Social Security will be taxed accordingly. The table above shows how one might calculate the amount of Social Security subject to taxation based on $30,000 in Social Security benefits and $45,000 in traditional IRA withdrawals.

Your objective, then, should be to avoid taxes on interest and dividends if possible. Tax-shelter your CDs and mutual funds. Better yet, reinvest your mutual fund money in index funds or separately managed accounts (more on this in the next chapter). Convert your tax-deferred accounts, like traditional IRAs, to tax-free accounts before you begin drawing Social Security. By enacting some or all of these strategies, you make sure that less of your money contributes to the chances of the IRS taxing your Social Security.

Non-reportable income, simply put, is any interest received on tax-deferred or tax-free accounts. Such interest does not fall under the IRS definition of ordinary income. It doesn't contribute to the aforementioned calculation. Non-reportable income includes gains paid on annuity balances which are typically tax-deferred. Also, interest on life insurance balances and Roth IRAs do not fall under reportable income because they are tax-free (read after-tax).

Earlier I mentioned phantom income—income that you may never see but that can add to your tax return. I like to call the result of phantom income, "torpedo taxes." To illustrate, imagine a couple named Bill and Michelle. They are in the 12% tax bracket. They both recently turned 72 and started collecting RMDs. The first RMD check was for $45,000. Based on their tax bracket, that means they'll pay $5,400 in taxes. Ah, but that's not all. Because of the distribution, the IRS kicks in taxes on $20,000 of their Social Security. At 12%, that results in an additional tax of $2,400 which they did not owe in previous years. The total taxes paid on their $45,000 RMD is $5,400 + $2,400 = $7,400 which makes for an effective tax rate of *17 percent*! That's the tax torpedo at work. Just for withdrawing their own money a certain way, Bill and Michelle are, for all intents and purposes, kicked up into a higher tax bracket.

"When Should I Start Withdrawing?"

At some point we need to ask this million-dollar question: "When will I start withdrawing from my Social Security benefits?" Your decision doesn't involve literally losing out on a million dollars, but it could mean the difference between a comfortable retirement and a miserable one.

There is no perfect answer to this question. Many people feel that you should begin withdrawing your benefits as soon as you can. Others say you should hold off as long as possible. The answer for you is probably somewhere in between. By taking some time to talk with a good financial advisor, you can find out what decision is best for your circumstances. You have to consider both sides of the coin. On one hand, the longer you wait the more you'll have. Your Social Security can grow by up to 8% every year you don't withdraw, until you're 72. On the other hand, you might need the money to retire before that age.

People who decide to begin their withdrawals at 62 usually do so for one of two reasons. One, they don't think they'll live long enough for their benefits to be worth the wait. Two, they think their benefits won't be there later. If you think you should start withdrawing for the second reason, you should reconsider your decision. The Social Security system in its current form is projected to last until 2035, and that's only if Congress doesn't take any action to bolster the system. Many experts expect change is on the horizon.

Many decide to withdraw at full retirement age – that is 67. I've found that those who decide to wait until this age or later are typically more informed and frugal. Some of my clients want to wait as long as they possibly can before they take their benefits. Sometimes they're the millionaires who still go out to eat at 4:30 to get a discount! They're the ones I have to tell to spend more.

Finding ways to maximize your Social Security benefits is a big part of retirement planning. The decisions you make have a huge effect on your retirement, and your life. I can't emphasize enough how critical it is that you consult a financial professional to help you to be wise with your Social Security benefits.

Chapter FOUR

Harness The Power Of Your Retirement Accounts

In the retirement world, 401(k)s and IRAs are almost as prolific as Social Security. These days, the 401(k) reigns as king of the mainstream retirement "plans." Unfortunately, a 401(k) is not much of a plan unto itself. It takes serious forethought to ensure that your 401(k) or IRA makes a sizable and stable contribution to your larger retirement plan.

Where Did The 401(k) Come From?

If you asked someone what a 401(k) was before the mid-1980s, you'd probably have been answered with a blank stare and a confused look. And yet, the idea for the 401(k) was born in a movement that started in the 1960s.

In 1963, the automobile manufacturer Studebaker filed for bankruptcy. Many companies fail to stay solvent, but Studebaker's demise was a unique case. When the company went under, it left over 20,000 employees – many of whom had worked on the factory line for decades – without a cent of their "guaranteed" pensions. Millions of dollars in pensions were gone overnight.

The United Automobile Workers (UAW), one of the country's most powerful labor unions, was horrified. For years, the organization had been lobbying for federal intervention to protect the interests of automobile workers, but its pleas had gone unnoticed. Now the UAW's worst nightmare had been realized. The Studebaker disaster validated concerns which the UAW had preached for years, and it gave the organization added leverage.

Walter Reuther, an outspoken civil and labor rights activist, had built the UAW into a force with which to be reckoned. But his vision of an amended pension system was naïve. In the heat of the UAW's battle for insured pensions, one pension expert told Reuther that the introduction of government involvement within the pension system would "reconfigure the 'incentives' of both labor and management." In other words, if the United States government was to address the pension problem, the entire system would have to change and the benefits which had always accompanied pensions would likely be slashed. Reuther couldn't have realized at the time how prophetic that warning would prove to be.

In 1974, the UAW's wishes were realized when Congress passed the Employee Retirement Income Security Act (ERISA). The act represented federal legislation to protect retirees and their assets. ERISA included the Pension Benefit Guaranty Corporation (PBGC) to insure private pensions. Then, in 1978, an obscure amendment to ERISA was tacked on. It was called the Revenue Act of 1978. It included a provision within the Internal Revenue Code (IRC) under Section 401, subsection (k), which allowed employees to avoid taxation on deferred compensation.

For a while, Section 401(k) went largely unnoticed. No one seemed to realize its potential until 1980. Ted Benna was a benefits consultant at the time. While researching ways to design tax-friendly retirement plans for a client, Benna stumbled upon IRC Section 401(k). It was exactly what he'd been looking for. Benna's idea was for employees to divert part of their earnings into a retirement account, pre-tax, while receiving an employer match.

Unfortunately, Benna's client rejected his idea, but he was confident he'd found a way to revolutionize retirement planning. Benna owned a company of his own, The Johnson Companies, which became the guinea pig for his 401(k) plan. The idea worked swimmingly. A year later, the IRS issued rules that allowed employees to fund their 401(k) directly from payroll deductions.

Thus the 401(k) was born. By 1983, about half of all major companies in the United States were introducing 401(k) plans to their employees.

IRA vs 401(k)

Plan type	IRA	401(k)
Account holder's contribution limit	$6,000	$19,500
Catch-up contribution limit for those aged 50 and older	$1,000	$6,500
Total contribution limit for those aged 50 and older	$7,000	$26,000
Maximum combined contribution for employee and employer	N/A	$57,000
Maximum combined contribution for employee and employer for those age 50 and older	N/A	$63,500

Individual Retirement Accounts

For much of this chapter, I may refer to 401(k)s and Individual Retirement Accounts (IRAs) interchangeably, but there are some fundamental differences. The biggest difference is that 401(k) plans are sponsored and managed by an employer while IRAs are self-directed. In other words, you may only contribute to a 401(k) while you are employed by the company offering it. Despite the restrictions imposed by 401(k)s, they offer the distinct advantage of employer contribution matching. If your employer matches everything you contribute to your 401(k), that's equivalent to 100 percent return on investment. It would take years to see the same growth from an IRA.

A second distinction between 401(k)s and IRAs is allowable annual contributions. The table on the previous page outlines contribution limits for IRAs and 401(k)s as of 2020.

Choices, Choices, Choices

If you're still in your working years, and you have not set up a 401(k), there are a few important decisions to consider. Your employer may offer a range of investments to choose from. They often include different mutual funds, or "default" offerings based on the risk tolerance you select. If you're young and willing to assume riskier asset allocations, you may choose a plan which includes target date funds. A target date fund is designed to reach a certain figure according to your retirement timeline. Fortunately, target date funds typically become more conservative as your retirement date nears to ensure that you are not subject to high risk with retirement on the horizon.

One of the biggest decisions you'll make when selecting a retirement account is to select a traditional or Roth account. With a traditional 401(k), any contributions you make to the account are withdrawn from your paycheck before tax and remain tax-free for the duration of your working years. Tax deferral introduces many appealing benefits. Many presume they will sit in a lower tax bracket after retirement. That means the money in their 401(k)s will owe less in taxes when they're finally due than if employees paid the tax up front. However, it can be dangerous to assume that you will be in a lower tax bracket after retirement.

A second benefit of a traditional 401(k) is that it has the potential to lower your taxes *now*. Since part of your income is withheld to fund your tax-deferred 401(k), that money does not contribute to your taxable income as it's interpreted by the IRS. If your income puts you near the bottom end of your tax bracket, there's a good chance that the subtraction of money for your 401(k) will be enough to drop you into a lower bracket.

Most employers offer traditional 401(k) plans and they remain the most popular retirement investment account. If you want to save on taxes now, a traditional 401(k) is probably the way to go. But there are also compelling reasons why you may want to pay taxes up front. If that's the case, a Roth account may be of interest to you.

Roth What?

The Roth construct was introduced in 1997. It was conceived by Delaware Senator William Roth. The eponymous retirement account has become a popular alternative to traditional 401(k)s and IRAs in the 20 plus years since its inception. But what sets Roth accounts apart from their traditional counterparts?

When Senator Roth first proposed the idea for an alternative version of the 401(k), his objective was simple: to make a retirement account that was tax-free by the time withdrawal would begin. But, of course, "tax-free" is never tax *free*. It's just a matter of when you have to pay your taxes. With a Roth account, you pay taxes up front – that is, upon contribution to the account – but interest accrued on the account is never taxed and taxes have been covered by the time you are retired and ready to withdraw income.

At first glance, a Roth 401(k) may appear to go back on what made 401(k)s unique. After all, tax deferral was the very thing Benna was looking for when he first devised the system. What's the point if you're just going to pay taxes up front anyway?

Roth accounts, like any investment type, are better suited to some investors than others. Personal circumstances will be the biggest determining factor in deciding between Roth and traditional 401(k)s and IRAs. If your circumstances allow, however, a Roth may yield striking benefits to your retirement plan.

For one thing, the stress of paying taxes on your retirement account is typically minimized with a Roth because you'll have the safety of a working income to cover those expenses. You may also spend less in taxes than with a traditional 401(k) if the income tax rate increases in the future.

Another benefit of a Roth account is the avoidance of Required Minimum Distributions (RMDs). When you turn 72, the United States government requires you to start withdrawing something from your traditional 401(k) or IRA. By 72, the government figures you've had long enough to benefit from tax deferral. Uncle Sam is hungry and he's ready for his cut. With a Roth, however, you paid your taxes already. He is satisfied, and you can let that money sit for as long as you'd like. If you're a bit late to the investment game, this feature can make Roth 401(k)s especially appealing. If you have income from other sources to sustain you, you can leave your Roth to grow with compounded interest even after having turned 72. Those extra years of growth can make a tremendous difference, especially if you're interested in leaving a sizable inheritance to your successors. If you retire at age 70 with $500,000 in a Roth account, it will grow to $1.2 million by your 85th birthday at six percent interest.

Finally, Roth accounts are beneficial for the added liquidity they offer over regular 401(k)s and IRAs. One investment group called Roth accounts a "retirement plan and an emergency fund in one." Unlike traditional retirement accounts which carry stiff penalties for early withdrawal, Roth accounts allow you to withdraw your money at any time for any reason.

In some cases, you might consider a Roth conversion. A conversion strategy allows you to transfer money from your traditional 401(k) or IRA to a Roth account. It does not require earned income and carries no limits on the amount to convert annually. That said, I do not recommend that an investor embark on a conversion strategy without the guidance of a financial professional. Without an intimate knowledge of tax and retirement planning, the average investor can get in trouble making Roth conversions.

Leaving The Workforce...Now What?

After many years in the workforce, you may have turned on cruise control with respect to your 401(k). Your contributions are probably automatic, and you may give the account little thought. But as retirement approaches

– or if you're leaving your job for another – it's time to make some important decisions.

There are essentially four options for your 401(k) when leaving your employer for another job, or to retire:

1. You can leave the money where it is.
2. You can take the cash.
3. You can transfer the money to another employer plan.
4. You can roll the money into a self-directed IRA.

I highly recommend that you consult with a financial professional before making a decision. The decision you make will undoubtedly impact your retirement plan. Many 401(k)s are closely connected to the company that offers and manages them. In some cases, it may not be possible to transfer a 401(k) from one employer to another 401(k) at your new job. On the other hand, some companies will not permit you to leave the money where it is. If you have changed jobs several times throughout your career and have several 401(k) plans in your possession, it may be wise to consolidate those funds in a self-directed IRA.

No matter what, though, you need to situate your 401(k) within a larger retirement plan. I too often sit down with new clients who have for many years considered their 401(k) to be a comprehensive retirement plan all by itself.

Should I Just Take The Cash?

When leaving a company, departing employees often have the option to take their 401(k) as a lump sum of cash. It may seem like the simplest option. However, for younger employees, cashing out a 401(k) can come with stiff penalties and exorbitant fees. For people underage 59 ½, withdrawing the contents of a 401(k) is typically met with fees from the investment management company, a 10 percent federal tax penalty, and the need to pay regular income tax.

There are, however, a few exceptions to the 59 ½ rule:

Exception to 59 ½ Rule	Applies to IRA or 401(k)
Death of Account Holder	Both
Total, Permanent Disability of Account Holder	Both
First-time Homebuyer (up to $10,000)	IRA
Higher Education Expenses	IRA
Unreimbursed Medical Expenses (limited)	IRA
Separation from Employer After Age 55	401(k)

If you are younger than age 59 ½ and the above exceptions do not apply to your situation, I don't recommend withdrawing cash from your 401(k). It's not uncommon for investors to realize only after withdrawing from their 401(k)s that nearly 20 percent has been forfeited in the way of taxes, fees, and penalties. Especially if you have the bulk of your retirement savings in 401(k)s, be weary of the 59 ½ rule. It can get you in trouble if an emergency arises.

These expenses and limitations make "in-service rollover" a much better option. This option allows you to transfer the funds from your 401(k) into an IRA without taking the funds as a distribution. You ditch the fees and other expenses that come with taking the cash. In-service rollover is an option that is almost always available. Choosing this course will give you confidence that your money is in a safe place.

Can I Still Stretch My IRA?

The "stretch IRA" was a strategy used in retirement and estate planning to pass the funds of an IRA from one generation to the next. It allowed many to minimize the taxes incurred from an inherited IRA. This strategy was very effective and was used by many financial professionals; in fact, I used to have an entire chapter in this book dedicated to the strategy. However, this method of passing on funds in an IRA has been changed by the SECURE Act.

The SECURE Act was passed in December of 2019. It has a variety of features and provisions, but the most notable involves inherited IRAs. Stretch IRA was founded on the notion of stretching the funds from an inherited IRA over decades of time. Now as a feature of this act, all funds from that IRA must be withdrawn within 10 years after the original holder of that IRA dies. The only exception is, of course, if the beneficiary is the spouse of the deceased.

So, if you've asked, "Can my IRA still be stretched?" The answer is still yes, but only for 10 years. Granted, 10 is better than zero. But you now need to use other strategies in your estate planning to ensure a lasting legacy.

Take Charge Of Your Retirement

When 401(k)s first gained popularity in the 1980s, they were hailed as the replacement to the outmoded pensions of old. After all, the 401(k) option was born of a movement to reform issues within the pension system. But it's a mistake to view 401(k)s and IRAs as a replacement for pensions. They are not a fair and equal trade.

Even Ted Benna, the man credited with introducing the 401(k) into the modern retirement planning world, takes issue with the way 401(k)s have evolved. According to an interview in 2018, Benna thinks the 401(k) "has gone awry." When asked to explain why he's been critical of 401(k) plans in recent years, Benna said their development has "not [been] a pretty picture. It went from all fees being paid by the employer to everything getting bundled and dumped on employees

Indeed, 401(k)s carry several fees and expenses which can be burdensome for the 401(k) owner. Besides that, 401(k) has always obligated employees to carry the burden of funding. Pensions are employer-funded. The money that funds a pension doesn't come from your paycheck; it's something extra contributed by the company you work for. But 401(k)s and IRAs are self-funded. That distinction has made a tremendous difference in the relative contributing power of 401(k)s to retirement compared to pensions. While many people have 401(k)s, very few have funded them well enough to supply the entirety of their retirement income.

According to a recent report by the Employee Benefit Research Institute (EBRI), the median amount in 401(k) accounts paints a bleak picture of retirement prospects.

$18,433 – that's how much the average person has in his or her 401(k). "Almost 40 percent of employees have less than $10,000, even as the proportion of companies offering alternatives like defined benefit pensions continues to drop," the report continues.

"Older workers do tend to have more savings," EBRI found, but not nearly enough to fund retirement on its own. The median for employees aged 55 to 64 was $76,381. "But even at that level," the report concludes, "millions of workers nearing retirement are on track to leave the workforce with savings that do not even approach what they will need for health care, let alone daily living. Not surprisingly, retirement is now Americans' top financial worry.

What does that mean for you? In short, don't put all your eggs in the 401(k) and IRA basket. They can make an excellent contribution to your retirement portfolio, but don't misconstrue a 401(k) for a complete retirement plan. Take care to ensure that your money is well diversified and protected with a variety of investment options working in tandem to produce a sustainable retirement income.

IRAs and 401(k)s have the potential to be powerful assets, but in my experience, I have found annuities to be even more powerful. I have access to some of the best annuities out there and have used them to help my clients build a strong retirement portfolio. What people don't realize is that good annuities are backed by more money than what most companies have to fund a pension or contribute to a 401(k). And with the right annuity, your money can be more liquid than it is with either an IRA or a 401(k). In chapter 10 of this book, we will discuss in detail how you can use annuities to build your own "pension."

Warren Buffet has always made the point that we should, 'hope for the best, but plan for the worst.' In the seminars that I hold, I've asked the question: "How many of you got a call from your broker or your financial advisor saying that the market was going to tank in 2008?" No one has ever raised their hand. We simply don't know what the future holds. You can use that as an excuse for bad planning or as a factor in a good plan. When we plan for the unknown, we put ourselves in a much better spot than if we didn't. We are prepared for the worst, even if it never comes.

Chapter FIVE

The Taxman Cometh

Another bandit hiding in the bushes along our highway to solid financial planning for retirement is the taxman. If you are like most people, you don't object to paying your fair share of taxes. You just don't like having to pay more than your fair share. But there are ways to keep from getting robbed if you simply give some attention to tax-managing your money. Keep in mind:

It's Not What You Make, It's What You Keep That Counts.

Now's a good time to ask this question:

What kind of stocks, bonds, mutual funds, and exchange-traded funds should we invest in? Below, you will see a chart showing the relative performance of market sectors. As you can see, the winning sector is different each year. What does that tell us? Simply this: no one knows! No one is smart enough or prescient enough to tell us which way the market will move or in what the ebb and flow of the numbers will result.

When it comes to purchasing a product, whether it is something major, like a new car or a home, or something minor, like a music CD, we often buy out of emotion and then defend the purchase, mainly to ourselves, with logic.

It is not much different when it comes to investing. Here, the emotion is the desire for gain. Some may call it "greed", but that is a little harsh. Regardless of what label you give it, this emotion often causes us to be errant in our judgment. People will buy a stock or a mutual fund when they hear it described as "hot," and then they sell in a panic when it inevitably drops in value.

Rick Elderman put it this way, "Stocks are not the problem... YOU are the problem because you let your emotions get in the way."

So, what's the fix?

Control Yourself

As we watch our 401(k)s lose 40 percent of their value, and we see the United States banking industry wobble, just reading the headlines can cause our blood pressure to rise and our fear factor to intensify. It can be a challenge not to act impulsively in our angst. After all, it's only human. "That's my hard-earned money on the line!" you may say when the charts take a nosedive.

When emotions become the overriding reasons for making investment decisions, we call that the "jungle instinct." Let's say you are on your own out in the jungle. You must survive in a dangerous and threatening environment. Your surroundings are hostile. There are predators about, and you are their prey. A branch snaps. You hear a growl. To your right is a tree with a low-hanging limb. To your left is a cliff, below which is a roiling river. You have a split second to act.

This is the time your jungle instinct kicks in. You make a quick decision, based on sketchy information with limited resources, impelled by heightened emotions to either flee, fight, or, in some cases, hide in order to survive.

Let's face it. That's okay for the jungle, but it doesn't work well when dealing with our finances. We need to resist the temptation to make quick, emotionally driven decisions. When the market is unpredictable and financial turmoil is the order of the day, it is a time to keep a cool head. Be analytical. It is a time to use, not only our brains, but also all the brainpower we can borrow, to accumulate the facts, obtain the correct analysis, and act accordingly. It is a time to focus keenly with a steady aim. Take the time to devise a tested strategy that works...one with which you are comfortable and one that fits you and your unique circumstances; and then act on it with deliberation. After devising that strategy, then implement it and stay the course until it pays off.

A subsequent chapter discusses taxes in greater detail—how to keep Uncle Sam from being the biggest beneficiary of your IRAs and 401(k). I will also go into depth on how to protect your estate from taxes in a tax landscape that is constantly shifting and is anything but predictable.

Chapter SIX

Tax-Free Retirement

Compound interest is like a snowball rolling downhill. As it gains momentum, the bigger it will get. Perhaps that is the reason the genius Albert Einstein reportedly called compound interest the "eighth wonder of the world"!

To illustrate the power of compound interest, let's say that in 1492, when Christopher Columbus discovered the New World, he found a penny. Being the smart guy that he was, he put the penny into an interest-bearing account yielding 6 percent compounded annually. Can you guess how much that penny would be worth today? Would you believe somewhere in the neighborhood of $145 billion?

But suppose Queen Isabella found out about the penny and levied a 3 percent annual tax on Christopher's investment? His penny would only be worth $8 million. To put that in perspective, a million seconds is twelve days. A billion seconds is thirty-one years. A million minutes ago was almost two years ago, whereas a billion minutes ago was just after the time of Christ.

So perhaps if Albert Einstein had an opportunity to study financial planning, he might have concluded that a tax-free retirement strategy may have been at least the fourth or fifth wonder of the world.

To put it more realistically, let's say that we have one dollar, and every year we can double it. Let's assume that we can double our dollar every year for twenty years. We are going to be millionaires! If we don't have to pay taxes, we will have $1,048,000 free and clear.

Now go back and say that we have to pay taxes on the money every year. Our $1,048,000 has shrunk to $57,000.

So how does tax-free retirement work?

Most of us are familiar with investment vehicles that are tax deferred; that is, we don't pay taxes on the earnings until we reach in and take the money out. This category includes such qualified plans as 401(k), 403(b), IRAs, SEPs, etc. They are called "qualified plans" because they qualify for special tax treatment under the IRS code.

Then there are investments on which the gains are taxable up front, such as stocks, mutual funds, real estate, CDs. You will pay capital gains tax on the earnings from these vehicles. Typically, short-term gains are taxed at the marginal income tax rate, and long-term gains are taxed at the going rate, which changes over time. Ordinary income tax rates, of course, are applied to regular income, and this rate, too, can change. Many predict, given the current economic climate of mounting national debt, that this rate will go higher in the near future.

In a tax-deferred plan, at retirement your contributions and gains will be taxed at your income tax rate. In a tax-free plan, at retirement, you will pay zero percent in taxes, because the gains are not taxable, and you have already paid taxes on your contributions.

What investment vehicles are available for tax-free retirement?

Roth IRA. The money put into a Roth IRA is taxed when you receive it, but it is not taxed when it is withdrawn, including investment earnings, in retirement. Unfortunately, there are income limits that exclude many people from being eligible to contribute to a Roth IRA. For those who are eligible, the annual contribution limit is six thousand dollars, or, if you are age fifty or over, seven thousand.

Roth 401(k) or 403(b) account. The IRS now allows you to make Roth contributions inside 401(k) and 403(b) accounts. This is an excellent feature if your plan allows it because withdrawals of the Roth contributions and earnings in retirement are tax-free. An individual age fifty or older can make a total contribution of up to twenty-two thousand dollars to a Roth 401(k) account, an amount that includes five thousand, five hundred dollars in catch-up contributions. Unlike the Roth IRA, there are no income eligibility limits. However, you will have to pay tax on the Roth contributions in the year you make the deposit, and Roth contributions will reduce the amount of traditional 401(k) contributions you can make.

Municipal Bonds and Funds. Income distributions from municipal bonds are not subject to federal income taxes. (They may be subject to state income taxes.) For this reason, the interest these bonds pay is generally lower than taxable bonds. If you buy and sell municipal bonds on the secondary market, any gain from those sales will be taxed as ordinary long or short-term capital gains. There are no income limits for this tax-free benefit.

Indexed Universal Life Insurance. With Internal Revenue codes such as 7702 and 72e we have the ability to accumulate cash within a permanent insurance policy as tax deferred. As long as the insurance contract is constructed within the TEFRA, DEFRA, and TAMRA guidelines, cash values can be withdrawn with no tax consequences. An IUL is linked to a market indicator or index, and then that credited interest is limited by a minimum guaranteed interest rate as well as a capped interest rate. This means you can enjoy the upside of the market without having to be involved in the downside. An IUL product still has all the traditional benefits and advantages of life insurance, but because of the above advantages also serves as a valuable engine for tax-deferred wealth accumulation.

Health Savings Account. This is one of my favorite ways to invest for tax-free retirement income. If your employer offers health insurance coverage using an HSA, the combined contributions by the employer and employee to the account can be as high as $7100 in 2020 (for a family plan) plus an additional $1,000 if you are age fifty-five or older. Unlike the other tax-free income options described above, HSA contributions are tax deductible and there are no income limits.

HSA funds are held by a plan administrator and can be invested for long-term growth. The investment options can vary from plan to plan. The employee can withdraw funds from the HSA to pay for (or reimburse) a wide variety of qualified medical expenses, including some expenses not covered by insurance. As long as you follow the rules on which expenses are reimbursable, no taxes are paid on withdrawals, including on investment gains. You can hold the HSA funds and earnings until you retire and use them to provide tax-free income by reimbursing yourself for past expenses and for current expenses, including Medicare premiums.

It is clear, then, with so many tax-free options available to those concerned about their retirement that any competent financial advisor would be doing his/her clients a disservice if he/she did not make clients aware of them.

Chapter SEVEN

Risk Tolerance Matters

Over the years, I have observed that good doctors spend much more time in the examination phase than they do in the diagnosis and prescription phase. And the more serious they think a problem may be, the more time they spend listening and asking questions before rendering a diagnosis or prescribing a remedy.

So when, in 2007 a seventy-two-year-old man walked into my office seeking financial advice, I instinctively took out my notepad and began listening and asking questions.

My visitor was tall and distinguished looking. He was casually dressed and gave the impression that he was quite intelligent, although not necessarily about money. He was a computer engineer who had worked for a highly respected local Internet company. He had been participating in the company's 401(k) plan since its inception, and to its credit, his company had contributed matching funds generously. The account had done well, especially during the boom years of the 1990s, and was worth over $750,000.

I scribbled notes as the man told me that he had been counting on his pension to see him through his retirement years. He said he felt quite secure he would not even have to touch his 401(k). He thought that his generous pension would be substantial enough to cover his living expenses. He had estimated that he would be able to live quite comfortably during his retirement, continue to let the money in his 401k and qualified accounts, such as his IRA, grow, and then pass that money along as an inheritance to his children. What he didn't know, however, and had no way of knowing, was that the Internet company where he had worked for all those years was in financial trouble. What prompted his visit to my office was that he had just that week learned that the company had declared bankruptcy, and his pension had been wiped out.

The more I listened as the man related his tale of woe, the more I began to discern that he was unknowingly sitting on another potential time bomb. He had relied on the advice of a stockbroker to manage the assets within the 401(k), and from the statements he shared with me, I could see that he was more than 90 percent at risk. I knew in principle he could fix that. But what neither of us knew, or could have known, was that, economically speaking, there were serious storm clouds brewing on the horizon. The housing bubble that had been building for almost a decade was soon to burst. The stock market would take a sudden free fall, and the unprepared would see as much as 40 percent of their fortunes go down the drain.

The Rule Of 100

Using the Rule of 100 when it comes to risk tolerance is as important, or should be, to financial planning, as using a level and a square to build a house. Put simply, it is this: you take the number one hundred and subtract your age from it, and what's left is the maximum you should have exposed to market risks. Let's say you are sixty years old. Then $100 - 60 = 40$. So, you should have 40 percent of your portfolio invested in the market. If you are age twenty-five, you should have 75 percent of your assets at risk in the market, invested for long-term gains. If you are seventy-two, like our distinguished gentleman who sat in my office, then no more than 28 percent of your assets should have been at risk in the market. Certainly not 90 percent.

The solution in this case was simply to rearrange this man's money to the balance required by the Rule of 100, which is what we did. Then, when the stock market lost $11 trillion in the seventeen months that began October 9, 2007, he was insulated from what would have been a devastating loss. Had he stayed 90 percent exposed, almost half of his wealth would have vanished. Because he heeded the tried-and-tested formulas for financial planning that made sense for him, he was able to continue living the lifestyle that he had previously enjoyed.

One of the most rewarding moments of my career came when I received a phone call from him to tell me that he and his daughter had just returned from China where they toured the famous Terracotta Army of Emperor Qin. He told me that had we not met and discussed the Rule of 100 and implemented the strategies we did; he could not have afforded to take the trip and would have missed the opportunity to forge such an unforgettable memory with his daughter. Some families have large accounts and want to reverse the 60/40 to 40/60 and add to the safe bucket as they get older to get more safety.

But what the phone call left me wondering was how many other fortunes could the Rule of 100 save? According to the statistics I have seen, the majority of Americans fail to start planning for retirement when they should. When people are age twenty-five, they are bulletproof and immortal, so there are not too many twenty-five-year-olds who have chunked away 75 percent of their assets into a stock market investment portfolio. I would venture to guess that they have instead placed those assets in cars and big screen TVs. Then there are seniors who are on the bottom of the accompanying triangle when they should be at the top. That is, they have portfolios with one of the major brokerage firms and are too heavily weighted in buy-and-hold scenarios that simply don't work in modern economic times. It's topsy-turvy!

Chapter EIGHT

The Three Phases Of Money

"The pessimist sees difficulty in every opportunity. The optimist sees the opportunity in every difficulty." - Winston Churchill

The other day I saw a clever illustration that was produced to show the progression of our lives from birth to death. It was a row of bottles, starting with a baby bottle, going to a coke bottle, a beer bottle, and finally a bottle of antacid medicine. Sad, but true! When it comes to how we view the acquisition, preservation and distribution of our money, there are basically three phases we will go through. See if you don't agree.

- **ACCUMULATION MODE**—These are our younger years when we are working hard to accumulate and save, invest, and earn. We can take greater risks because we have time to ride the ridges and troughs of the economic waves that wash over us during these years. Although there is always an ebb and a flow, the end result has always been historically on the upside. Take any fifteen-year slice of the S&P, for example, and the average gain is in the neighborhood of 8 percent. That statistic is very dependable. In other words, start in 1958 and go forward fifteen years to 1973 and measure the results, and there will be a gain of around 8 percent. Go from 1975 to 1990, and the gain will be in the same neighborhood.

- **PRESERVATION MODE**—Here are the years when you begin thinking about retirement. Some of your friends have already retired. What were dreams twenty years ago have come to fruition because you have worked hard, and you have been a good saver and a careful investor. The goal now is not to lose it by getting caught in one of those troughs and you simply don't have enough time to catch the next wave up. Your challenge now is to hold on to what you've got and make decisions that will ensure it will last the rest of your life.

- **DISTRIBUTION MODE**—Now it's time to enjoy your hard work by spending your money. Spend it as judiciously as the situation you have created for yourself warrants but use it to maintain the lifestyle to which you have become accustomed and to keep your independence. The key here is to allow it to continue growing without significant risk while you rake off what you need to accomplish the above.

"May The Force Be With You"

You may or may not remember this from your high school physics classes, but it was Sir Isaac Newton who came up with the law of inertia. Actually, I don't think Sir Isaac actually "came up" with it. He was just the first one to identify and explain it. "And just what does that have to do with finance?" you ask.

The law of inertia simply states that an object in motion will stay in motion until something pushes it or pulls it in another direction. It's the same way for sitting still. An object that is stationary will continue to just sit there until an outside force makes it move.

When it comes to money decisions, all of us are affected by the law of inertia to some degree. We are all a bit resistant to change. If you don't believe this, try this experiment. Analyze which leg you put into your trousers or pants first. Next morning, start using the other leg first.

So, we don't easily move from one mode to the other. Sometimes we have to be jolted out of our comfort zone.

Take moving from the accumulation mode to the preservation mode for example.

During the accumulation mode, we made a lot of money. We liked that. It was exciting. But we also lost a lot of money when those market corrections happened, didn't we? That wasn't fun, but we hung in there because we knew that in time it would come back, and it always did. In the 1990s the stock market made tremendous gains. The strategy of "buy and hold" worked quite well. Heck, in the latter part of that decade practically any strategy worked. As one investor said of that era, "I could do no wrong!" One of the most amazing periods was the time from January 1990 to March 1990 when the market grew an astonishing 455 percent. People were streaming to this new American bonanza in droves. Companies were starting up 401(k)s, and all of this money had to be parked somewhere. The market swelled so swiftly that a certain euphoria overtook the nation. Many thought it would never end. But indeed, it did. On March 24, 2002, the correction began and $9 trillion was lost in thirty months. Had you had $455,000 in the market, it would have dropped to $231,595, and $100,000 would have turned into $50,900. If you retired in March of 2000, you would have seen a 49.1 percent decline in your retirement nest egg.

So, is "buy and hold" for the long term the answer in today's market? No. Even if you could count on there being a steady 10 ten percent gain each year with no losses, which is unrealistic to the point of being silly to even contemplate, it would still have taken eighty-two months for your account to just break even and get back where you started. At a steady 5-percent growth, it would have taken 161 months to just break even.

What happened next? From October 9, 2002, to October 9, 2007, the stock market went up, up, up! We had a 102 percent return during that period. Your $50,900 would have grown to $102,818! Not bad, right?
But then what happened on October 9, 2007? As was mentioned earlier, we had an $11 trillion decline. The Dow Jones lost 53.7 percent, and the S&P 500 lost 56.7 percent. Now your $100,000 is valued at $44,520. Do we see a pattern here?

The definition of a bear market is one where there is a decline of 20 percent or more. Since 1929, these bear markets occurred every 4.8 years. That's the average. There is no way of pinpointing when they will occur or how long they will last.

The average depth of a bear market is a 38.24 percent drop. The average duration of a bear market is seventeen months. The average time it would take to make up losses in a bear market is sixty months.

So that's why we say that a buy-and-hold strategy just doesn't work in today's economic environment. Managing a market portfolio successfully today requires going to the strongest asset at any given time. In 2008, the strongest asset was cash. Successful money managers will not fear going mainly to cash when the situation calls for it. We are happy to report that on the money-management side of our firm, we were able to forestall significant losses for our clients by moving them to a mostly cash position. This is not a commercial, or an attempt to toot our own horn. It simply illustrates how vital it is to make informed decisions based on tried-and true-methods of money management.

It is important that both the fundamental as well as the technical sides of the analytical spectrum be looked at in order to decide where to position the assets of clients. What does that mean?

In financial analysis, the fundamental side can be likened to a movie review where the critic says the picture is horrible; whereas the technical side promotes the same "horrible" movie as being such a popular hit that the ticket lines go down the street and around the block. So, while past performance cannot guarantee future results, you may be able to avoid the full brunt of a major downturn by using tools to identify trends. If the major downturn doesn't happen overnight, you may be able to reduce your exposure ahead of time.

So, it is just wise to weigh your individual risk tolerance carefully, taking into consideration your age and your financial goals. That way you can sleep at night, knowing that, regardless of what the market does or doesn't do, your retirement nest egg won't vanish overnight.

Chapter NINE

Different Kinds Of Money

There are three different kinds of money with which we need to plan:

- **EMERGENCY MONEY**—This is money we can put our hands on right now for any emergency that may come along. This is liquid cash, and it is probably going to be placed in an account where it is available and retrievable upon demand, like a checking or savings account or perhaps even a short-term CD. It is recommended that you have enough emergency money on hand to represent between three- and six-month's income. Like I said, it's for emergencies, so how much you deem is enough depends on your imagination as to what kind of situation may present itself. It certainly would be an emergency if you suddenly lost your job in the peak of your accumulation years. Because this money is for emergencies, it must be as liquid as possible, which means that it may not be earning a lot of interest, but don't worry about that. The key is that you will be able to access it immediately when you need it.

- **INCOME-PLANNING MONEY**—This money will be working for us, sure. In fact, we need it to produce a substantial rate of return for us since we are using this chunk of money for our retirement. But it must be safe from the possibility of loss. Since you will be using this money to provide a fixed lifetime income for you and your spouse, let's call this our "fixed income" account. We need market-like returns, but we can't put this money in the stock market because it could be lost in a sudden downturn. We need this money to be as safe as it would be if it were, for example, in a bank. But the banks don't pay very much interest, do they? So where does that leave us? We will discuss that after I mention the third type of money below.

- **INVESTMENT MONEY**—This money is money that, while we don't want to lose any of it, we need to have at risk. If the amount in this account is appropriate to our age, as previously discussed, we can afford to have this money at somewhat of a risk so as to produce the reward that is commensurate with that risk and thus balance out our financial plan. Remember, we have already salted away our emergency money. We already have our income-planning money working for us on what amounts should be on automatic pilot. This investment money has to roll up its sleeves and get to work in an actively managed program that changes with the ebb and flow of an ever-changing marketplace.

Now that we have identified these three types of money, let's answer the question that I know is on your mind. How in the world do we take the number two type of money, income-planning money, and pull off the trick of having it completely safe but at the same time generate better-than-average returns?

There are only so many places you can put your money.

Three Investment Worlds

SAFE	LINKED	RISK
Banks – Certificate of Deposit (CDs)		Stocks
Government – Treasury Bond	Fixed Index Annuity (FIA)	Mutual Funds
Insurance – Fixed Index Annuity (FIA)		Bonds
		Exchange-Traded Funds (ETF)
		Real Estate Investment Trusts (REIT's)
		Variable Annuities (VA)
Safe from Stock Market	Safe from Stock Market	Not Safe from Stock Market
No Growth	Potential Growth	Potential Growth

You will notice on the left side of the chart, there are only three places you can put money where it is guaranteed to be safe:

- banks
- government
- insurance companies

Banks—They mainly offer checking accounts, savings accounts, and certificates of deposits. These accounts are insured, in most cases up to $200,000 per account, by the FDIC. So, they are very safe.

Government—The government offers bonds...savings bonds, treasury bonds, municipal bonds, and the like. These are as safe as the governmental entity that provides them. The U.S. government is the only agency of which I am aware at the present time that has the authority to actually print money.

Insurance Companies—They offer fixed annuities, which have a fixed interest rate similar to that of a bank. Purely fixed annuities are safe from market risk but typically have low growth rates.

On the right side of the chart, we have the places to put your money that involve varying degrees of risk:

- stocks
- mutual funds
- bonds
- exchange traded funds
- real estate investment trusts
- variable annuities

By the way, variable annuities typically have anywhere from 3 to 5 percent in fees. When you hear people say, "Watch out for annuities with high fees," they are invariably referring to variable annuities, not fixed annuities. As opposed to fixed annuities, variable annuities are not safe from market risk. But there is a possibility of excellent growth.

Notice that in the middle of the Safe/Risk Chart there is another column: the banks needed to make CDs more attractive. They found a way by linking the account to an index like the S&P 500 to have better returns with a cap and a floor so that they remain safe with better returns. Government bonds followed suit with TIPS and then fixed indexed annuities were invented. These are relatively new instruments that are rapidly growing in popularity. Billions of investment dollars have gone into these since 1995. These became popular with IRA money because of the safety with market-like returns.

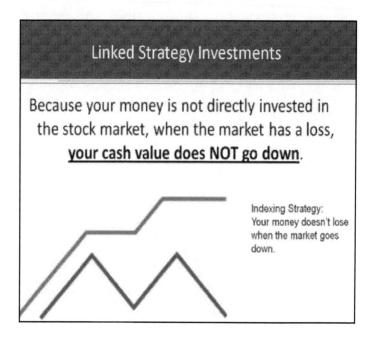

- 62 -

Creating Your Own Pension

If you were asked the question, "Do you have a pension in your retirement future?" you might say, "No. But I wish I did!" The sad truth is pensions are few and far between. But what if I told you that you could create your own pension? That might sound too good to be true. But it isn't. How is it possible? One word: Annuities.

By taking advantage of the newfound power of annuities you can, in effect, create a pension. A pension is a regular payment made to an individual who retires. It is sponsored by that individual's employer and guarantees a certain amount of money each month. The kinds of annuities that we are going to discuss are not sponsored by an employer, but they offer the same benefits as pensions and are founded on similar terms.

This idea of using annuities to create an asset similar to a pension might sound crazy, or even frightening. After all, aren't annuities unstable? You've probably heard the horror stories of archaic annuities crumbling, leaving people's lives in shambles. But I'm here to tell you, annuities have changed.

Annuities are similar to cars. They seem to get better every year. Better gas mileage, more high-tech options, plusher carpet, nicer upholstery. Annuities have undergone similar improvements to meet the financial needs, wants, and desires of today's consumers. Remember this old commercial from years ago? "This isn't your Father's Oldsmobile"? The same goes for annuities. These aren't your father's annuities. Today, you are likely to find much better guarantee options with higher returns than you would have ten years ago.

The Pension Of The Future

Annuities are insurance products designed to pay you a fixed sum in the future with money that is set aside today. While pensions have been praised for their strength and survivorship, they *are* annuities by definition, because of their payment structure. They can suffer from the same issues as an annuity plan that you set up for yourself. That simple truth about the pensions of today and yesterday, points us to the pension of the future. While fewer employers want to guarantee pensions, the benefits they provide are just as desirable now as they were decades ago. So, what is the solution? Create your own pension!

You might think that only a pension can guarantee 100% spousal benefit, and only a pension can guarantee 100% benefit to your kids. But that isn't true. I have helped my clients to find annuities that can guarantee these very same benefits. In fact, nine out of 10 of my clients have been able to get an extra $1000 or more a month by rolling over funds from an employer-sponsored annuity into another annuity, without any extra fees. I can help you carefully craft an annuity plan that gives you all of this. While there are a few exceptional pensions that can't be beat, I've been successful in helping my clients to develop annuities that are just as strong – if not stronger – than pensions. This lets them soar through their retirement with more than they ever expected.

Fixed Or Variable?

In the world of annuities, there are fixed, and there are variable annuities. They are as different as chocolate is from vanilla.

The standard fixed annuity promises a fixed rate whereas the variable annuity will be pegged to a riskier investment, such as mutual funds or stock-market indices. When compared to other safe-money alternatives, such as savings accounts, money markets, bond funds, and certificates of deposit, fixed annuities may just offer some of the highest fixed rates available. Some even include nursing care and terminal illness provisions, which will be very useful in the event you need to access all of your money in an emergency and pay no penalty for the privilege of doing so. For those investors who want no possibility of loss, fixed annuities are still considered to be the safest option. Variable annuities hold out the possibility of higher returns on your investment but have no guarantees that you won't lose your principal because of stock-market losses. So, for retirees, variable annuities are a bit risky, and I generally do not recommend that they own one.

To continue with the ice-cream analogy, the fixed indexed annuity (FIA), is, I suppose, chocolate with sprinkles and nuts, and, if you add the income rider, a cherry on top.

Here are how others describe the FIA:

"The Fixed Indexed Annuity can be confusing, but they can be valuable savings plans." —*Ernst & Young*

"The returns of the fixed indexed annuity are based on the returns of an equity market index, such as the S&P 500 where the principal investment is protected from losses in the equity market when gains add to the annuity's return."
—*Insured Retirement Institute*

"An indexed annuity is a fixed annuity, either immediate or deferred, that earns interest or provides benefits that are linked to an external equity reference or an equity index. The value of the index might be tied to a stock or other equity index. One of the most commonly used indices is the S&P 500, which is an equity index.... When you buy a fixed indexed annuity, you own an insurance contract. You are not buying shares of any stock or equity index."
—*National Association of Insurance Commissioners Buying Guide*

Viewed In A Different Light

As some of you know, some of these products were widely criticized prior to 2008 and then heavily praised in the wake of the economic events that year. They were criticized largely because they were said to be difficult to understand. The greatest wave of praise for them came in the wake of the severe drop in the stock market in 2008 when it was observed that these products protected investors from those losses.

It is interesting to note how these products have become more mainstream and consumer friendly. We suggest that you find an independent advisor who is not working for any particular insurance company or investment firm, but one who has a world of choices at his/her disposal to recommend. Most importantly, select an advisor who is required by law to maintain a fiduciary relationship between himself or herself and the clients. That way the advisor is duty-bound to put your interests ahead of his or her own. Examine different annuity contracts from several of the companies who design and sell them. Find the one that matches your individual financial circumstances.

Avoid The Downturns

Have you lost money in the market? Most have. But consider this: if you had invested ten dollars in the U.S. stock market in 1928 and held it until 2002, you would have $10,957 today. Let's imagine you happened to miss the thirty best months of the market. Your investment would now be worth only $154. What would be the case if you missed the thirty worst months? Your ten-dollar investment would now be worth $1,317,803.

What am I trying to say? Simply that when it comes to long-term compounding, it is critical to focus on avoiding the worst periods. Why? Because stock valuations tend to fall faster than they tend to go up, and they seem to operate in a compressed time period. For example, using the same scenario as shown above, if you miss the thirty worst months and the thirty best months, your initial investment would be $18,558. This is 80 percent higher than the old buy-and-hold strategy. It is important, then, to calculate risk/reward evaluations based on the chance of losing money rather than solely on the chance of making money.

Interestingly, fixed-indexed annuity strategies have principal guarantees so that you cannot lose in a down year. Yes, the returns are tied to market indices, such as the S&P, Dow Jones, or NASDAQ, but since the bad months do not count against you and the returns are locked in, your money is not at risk.

Not only are your gains in these products tax deferred; there are also no management fees in these products, because there is no management taking place. Yes, your returns are linked to the performance of the market, but not actually in the market, thus no risk. So, no management fees are required. When returns are based on an index, they are easy to calculate: Where was the S&P 500, for example, at the beginning of your investment year, and where was it at the end of that twelve-month period of time? Your growth will be measured and credited up to the cap in that product.

How Do Income Riders Work?

How do the income riders work? The income rider is an option. For what is usually a miniscule fee deducted from the returns, a provision can be added to the contract that will add a whole new dimension to the term "income planning." The rider creates a separate account within the framework of the annuity that can be counted upon to provide a pension either immediately or at a point in the future of the owner's choosing. Typically, this separate account is guaranteed to grow at a rate of anywhere from 6–8 percent per year as it defers for retirement. In most contracts, compound interest is used. In some others, simple interest is used.

Either way, from our point of view, such guarantees are quite comforting to those who must count on their nest egg to get them through their golden years. Once the income is started, it will continue for the life of the annuitant and his or her spouse if that election is made. Taking the lifetime payout is not annuitizing the contract, upon death, the full value goes to heirs in most contracts. Some of the largest insurance companies offering this type of rider make a provision within the contract that doubles the pension for a specific period of time if nursing home care is needed. This is done without losing the element of having the payout extend for life. This is an indemnity provision. Translation: no bills are required, only a doctor's statement that two of the six activities of daily living cannot be performed by the annuitant. In other words, there are no strings attached. The money can be used for anything.

This certainly fits into the category of **S**leep **W**ell **A**t **N**ight (SWAN) planning for many retirees whose slumber might be restless without those guarantees. An added benefit to this approach is this: now that you have locked in place a pension-like guaranteed income for the rest of your life, you will feel comfortable attending to other investments, perhaps taking some risks that you otherwise would not have.

Professor David Babbel, of the esteemed Wharton School at the University of Pennsylvania, set forth the value of annuities with this statement: "Lifetime Income Annuities may not be the perfect financial instrument for retirement, but when compared under the rigorous analytical apparatus of economic science to other available choices, the retirement income where risk and returns are carefully balanced, they dominate anything else in most situations. It is the best way we have now to provide for retirement."

The Center for Retirement Research in Boston recently stated that "65% of U.S. households are now at the risk of not having enough money to sustain their standard of living in retirement."

What About The 4 Percent Rule?

Some financial planners abide by what they call the 4 percent rule, which they see as an alternative to an annuity. But how risky is it? The theory is that you build your portfolio during the accumulation period, and then, when in retirement, steadily withdraw 4 percent per year for living expenses while the remainder continues to grow. But that strategy had, and still has, many shortcomings according to those who study the world of retirement-income planning. According to the accounting firm of Ernst & Young, which tracks retirement income products, most of the old-world approaches and tools to manage retirement portfolios are based on models where certainty is implied and tradeoffs are dismissed.

The 4 percent rule holds that if a retiree has a portfolio which consists of, let's say 50 percent stocks and 50 percent bonds, then the retiree need not purchase an annuity, but can initially withdraw 4 percent of the assets to provide income and then increase the amount withdrawn in subsequent years to account for inflation. Proponents of this approach maintain that it will still give the retiree a 90-percent chance of having enough money for a thirty-year retirement without running out. These financial planners define this approach as a "conservative" one. I disagree vigorously. It has major flaws. One fundamental flaw is that the income is not guaranteed. Another flaw is that it doesn't fit the Rule of 100. Far too much money is at risk past the accumulation years. What if the projections of this at-risk period are unsustainable? Losses in the earlier years of retirement tacked on regular withdrawals raise the chance of failure dramatically.

T. Rowe Price has done some credible research in this area. Based on a 45 percent stocks/55 percent bond ratio and 4 percent annual withdrawals rising with inflation, the study concludes that, with negative annualized returns in the first years of retirement, there is a whopping 57 percent chance of failure—running out of money—in thirty years. "Moreover," the study continues, "such significant losses are not as aberrational as some might think."

So, what conclusions can we draw from all of this? We must quantify our risk when it comes to income planning. And, while you are doing so, don't forget to account for our old pal, Mr. Inflation, who is as dangerous as a black ninja. If you aren't looking for him, you won't see him until it's too late.

If you are at the end of your accumulation phase of dealing with your money, it is as if you are at the top of a long, hard climb. Congratulations! You made it. But, as all skilled mountain climbers know, the downhill side is much more treacherous than the ascent. Careful planning is essential if you are to survive. The trip on the reverse side will require some serious risk management if you are to make it down safely. Maybe risk avoidance would be a better strategy. We certainly don't want to adopt a wish-and-hope countenance at this juncture of our financial lives.

Our plan actually has to work. Simply put, retirees and those approaching retirement can't afford to make the mistake of risking what they cannot lose.

The Retirement Window

In all of this, there is such a thing as the retirement-transition window, which is probably five to ten years on either side of the actual date you hang up your spurs.

This is the time when it is imperative not to make mistakes. It is during this phase of your life that it is more important to recognize danger and ward off money-management errors than it is to reach for the highest investment returns. The key during this period is to maximize the rewards of success and minimize the consequences of failure. Return *of* capital must trump return *on* capital during this critical period. There can be no doubt that the need of financial instruments that contain provisions for guaranteed income is absolute during this phase. The recent market turmoil has clearly established that it is much more important to have a guaranteed income in retirement than merely accumulating a large retirement nest egg. True retirement security will require a sustainable strategy for preserving that nest egg and allocating it in such a way to meet one's own goals, plans, and dreams. Such a strategy demands the use of income annuities for nearly all retirees. Those approaching retirement with substantial retirement savings should consider preparing for retirement and preserving their principle with a deferred annuity that would provide a guaranteed sustained income that cannot be outlived.

Volatile Markets

"Rule #1: Never Lose Money"
-Warren Buffet

"Rule #2: Never Forget Rule #1"

Chapter ELEVEN

Why Use The New Hybrid Linked Annuities In Portfolios?

These days, it seems investors are looking for safety and security more than ever, especially after the major stock market corrections witnessed in 1999–2002 and 2007–2009. Many who have brokerage accounts and variable annuities still have not recovered their losses from those market downturns. What makes it even worse is that many of those folks were counting on those accounts to fund their retirement!

So, it is easy to understand the appeal of the fixed indexed annuity, or FIA. It was designed to provide a greater return than the traditional fixed annuity and to be a reliable alternative to a brokerage account. FIAs have been around since the mid-nineties, and already trillions of dollars have been deposited in them.

As to what they are and how they work, let's dissect the name.

- FIXED—These annuities are called "fixed" in that they are characterized as fixed annuities by the departments of insurance in each state. To some degree, they resemble the traditional fixed annuities since the investor's money is completely safe from market risk. The investor, usually called the "owner" or the "annuitant" in these types of contracts, does not actually own any stocks, securities, bonds, mutual funds, or any other equity that could potentially go down in value. But while FIAs have some of the positive attributes of the traditional fixed annuity, there are many ways in which they do not resemble the traditional fixed annuity at all.

- INDEXED—This word "index" is there because the rate of interest with FIAs is determined by a market index, like the S&P 500, the NASDAQ, or the Dow Jones, or even a combination of these and other indices, depending on how you set it up. This is different from the traditional fixed annuity, which has a declared rate of interest, usually set every year by the insurance company. With FIAs, the owner can choose among any number of crediting options within the contract that can allow him to tweak and adjust the way interest is accrued. But the basic principle is this: When the index goes up, so does your account value. When the index goes down, you can't go below zero. Proponents of this strategy, in fact, like to use the expression: "Zero is your hero in a down market."

- ANNUITY—It's an annuity. Under the definitions given to this particular financial instrument by both the state departments of insurance under which they are governed and the insurance industry itself, its designation is that of an annuity. And while FIAs have been around since the mid-nineties and are a variation on the annuity theme, we must still consider the fact that, like the traditional annuities, FIAs are tax deferred. Typically, taxes are only paid on these contracts when the owner reaches in and pulls money out. Also, like most other annuities, while in deferral, you are typically allowed to withdraw a generous amount of your funds from the contract without paying surrender penalties. Most contracts allow for 10 percent free withdrawals. Most FIAs are also RMD friendly. (The Internal Revenue Service imposes a Required Minimum Distribution after the annuitant reaches the age of seventy-two years, and this withdrawal is usually penalty free as well.) It is worth mentioning here that many annuities allow for larger distributions if the owner is confined to a nursing home or is terminally ill.

So, in what other ways is the FIA unlike its predecessor, the traditional fixed annuity? We have already mentioned the fact that a market index is used to determine interest as opposed to the declared rate set by the insurance company. But one hallmark difference is the manner in which these instruments can guarantee a lifetime income to the retiree without his having to annuitize. In other words, the retiree can be collecting this self-created, self-directed pension while the remainder of the money in the account is still his and still grows.

How does this work? Something called an "income rider" for fixed annuities was developed in 2005. This rider can be added to these contracts that will provide an income account that guarantees growth of approximately 7–8 percent, while the account defers for retirement. If we do the math that means this income account can double in as few as nine years. At some point, the annuitant turns on the pension, and it continues as long as the annuitant and spouse lives. Upon their deaths, the full remaining value of the account goes to the heirs. Many financial advisors feel that now, at last, they have the piece of the puzzle in place that will allow for true SWAN (**S**leep **W**ell **A**t **N**ight) retirement planning. Why? Because after we know the pension-like payout is in place for life, then other investment opportunities may be considered without the hand-wringing and sleepless nights that may come with market risk.

Behind The Clock Face

Even a clockmaker, when asked what time it is, will not usually take a watch apart while providing the answer. But there are those who feel comforted knowing how FIAs work behind the scenes. This is especially true of those who feel like a solution to such a prevalent problem in retirement is just somehow too good to be true.

So, here's how the gears of this program work:

Typically, in order to guarantee that there will be no losses incurred in annuities, the insurance company places the principal of an annuity in safe investments, such as bonds. The insurance company then takes the yield or interest earned on these safe investments and buys options in a particular index, like the Dow Jones, S&P 500, or the NASDAQ. After a period of time, usually one year, when the option contract comes due, one of two things will happen. If the market index has advanced, the option is cashed in, and the interest is then credited to the annuity principal. If the market has retreated, the option expires, and no interest is credited to the account for that year.

In practice, the annuity either gains or maintains value each year, but the investment cannot lose value due to negative market fluctuation. It is important to note that most FIAs have a minimum guarantee associated with their returns. But this safety net is seldom needed.

In the menu of options available to owners of these kinds of annuities is the fixed- interest option. This can be used when the account holder decides not to let the market index determine the interest credited in a particular year, but would rather take the lower, but guaranteed, fixed interest rate offered by the insurance carrier.

How do these annuities perform? In years where the broader markets have performed well, so have the fixed indexed annuities. More importantly, the crucial value of these types of accounts has been that they have maintained their principal as well as the interest gained from past years even during the rapid market declines we have seen recently.

Ernst & Young recently prepared on behalf of the non-profit group, Americans for Secure Retirement, an independent study entitled "Retirement Vulnerability of New Retirees." It had this to say: "Without additional guaranteed lifetime income streams, such as income provided by an annuity, middle-income Americans are at high risk of outliving their financial assets and living their final years in poverty."

Our response to that is one word: "Ditto,"

In any case, we hope these facts do explain the recent popularity of FIAs among individuals looking to preserve a lifetime's worth of hard work in an unstable market atmosphere. In a capitalistic society, the will of the consumer is irrepressible. With so many consumers looking for safety and security without having to sacrifice reasonable returns, it is no wonder that such a flood of money is gushing toward these financial instruments. Coming downstream with that current are many who are approaching retirement, or are in retirement, who want a guaranteed income along with the peace of mind that comes from knowing their investments cannot decline, which is why we endorse the idea of them placing a portion of their retirement dollars into a fixed indexed annuity.

Why Were FIAs Developed?

The old axiom, "necessity is the mother of invention" certainly applies when it comes to the financial industry. Going all the way back to ancient times when the barter system was in place, I can just imagine that those who collected taxes for the king must have noticed that these taxes were hard to collect in pigs and chickens! So, a coin was produced, with the ruler's likeness stamped on it. Of course, the coin could represent the value of such things as livestock, land, or produce. *Presto!* The modern monetary system was born. What a relief that must have been for those folks who didn't want to tote pigs and chickens around.

In the mid-nineties, with the baby boomers coming of age and for the first time beginning to think about retirement, there were very few options available to them that would give them both growth and safety.

The old-style annuities were not flying off the shelves at the annuity store. They simply weren't appropriate for many investors. High fees and low returns were a turnoff for the boom generation. Another definite factor that kept them from being used as a practical retirement tool was the fact that with the older annuities, the only way to get your money out was to annuitize, which created the ultimate good news/bad news situation. The good news is that you could turn your nest egg into an income that you could not outlive. But the bad news was that once you did that, you now lost control over the account. If you died, the insurance company kept the money. What was needed was not a good news/bad news situation, but a win/win situation.

This need caused the industry to put on their collective thinking caps. The first invention was the fixed indexed annuity, which for the first time allowed for interest crediting based on a market index, but only the ups of the ticker, and none of the downs. Next came the development of the income rider that could provide a pension-like payout without requiring the annuity owner to commit "annuicide" to receive it. (By committing annuicide I mean making that deal where you get a fixed, lifetime income from the insurance company, but if you die early the insurance company gets to keep the money).

So, if you had asked me twenty years ago for my advice on buying an annuity, I would have probably advised against it. But with the changes they have undergone in recent years, I have changed my mind and so have many other financial advisors.

We see more and more articles from reputable sources these days pointing out how effective certain annuities can be included in a well-thought-out retirement plan. Organizations such as Putnam Investments and the Government Accountability Office, who monitor the financial world, suggest that retirees have no more than 5–25 percent of their portfolios at risk in the stock market and the rest should be placed in annuities. The same advice is now even coming from the segment of the financial world that sells equities. They observe that, since retirees need less risk and more guarantees, annuities with guaranteed minimum withdrawal benefits provide savings for retirement with some degree of protection.

Annuities are still not a perfect fit for every investor, but the ones that can be used to create retirement income streams that will mirror a pension are being implemented by advisors with fiduciary requirements on an ever-increasing basis day by day. Depending on your overall situation and your desire for a guaranteed retirement income, you may wish to consider taking a lump sum from your savings and buying an annuity, which would give you regular payouts in retirement, just like a pension.

Chapter TWELVE

Is It Safe?

A few weeks after the stock market crash of 2008, I was scheduled to speak at a Financial-planning workshop. The title of my speech was "How Inflation Affects Retirement." But sensing that my audience was noticeably, and understandably, nervous and worried about what was going on with the economy, I scrapped the speech and just opened it up to questions...and there were several.

"Why didn't my broker see it coming?"
"Will the market go any lower?"
"Is the market going to recover?"
"Where should I put my money now?"

Because I am neither a fortune-teller nor a soothsayer, I had to say, "I don't know" to questions like that. Can you imagine how much in demand I would be if I could predict bull markets, bear markets, and stock market crashes? But the answer, "I don't know," while truthful, still felt a little hollow to me. In my practice, I deal with many retirees, and I am a proponent of safe-money investments. So, I could honestly say that none of my clients took a bath in the market tumble. But that fact was of little consolation to some in this audience who had seen their fortunes reversed by as much as 40 percent almost overnight. Their faith had been shaken. I could read it in their eyes. It was no wonder that they were looking for answers; each day jolted by newspaper headlines revealing cracks in what they thought was a pretty stout economy. Each day they were hearing of yet another government bailout. Institutions they had always considered to be rock-solid, like the big banks and General Motors, were now appearing, hat in hand, before congress asking for what amounted to a handout from Uncle Sam.

Just How Safe Are Insurance And Annuity Companies?

Traditionally, throughout the years, most analysts acknowledge that while all manner of other companies around may fall into financial trouble, insurance companies are set apart from such difficulty. And this is true. But few understand the reasons why.

In 2008, when Bear Stearns, Lehman Brothers, and Wachovia were on the ropes, some of the insurance giants also experienced huge losses on their investments. The price of their stock shares declined, and private investors, looking for a good return, stepped in to take up the slack.

But both independent analysts and other officials all agree that insurance companies are in no danger of going the way of the extinct banks. They assert, and rightly so, that policyholders and owners of annuities

are in no danger of being unable to receive the full value of the services and returns that their contracts promise them.
Why?

In a word, regulation.

Unlike the banks that collapsed or merged under pressure or had to line up for bailout money, insurance companies are tightly *regulated*, mostly by the states. Companies that offer annuity contracts, for example, are required to keep vast sums of cash and short-term, safe-as-cash investments to be able to uphold their contracts. In order to maintain their charters of operation, insurance companies must comply with state audits that make sure they are fully capable of maintaining these funds in sufficient amounts to do this.

Another regulation provision that should make those with insurance company contracts **S**leep **W**ell **A**t **N**ight is that insurance companies are required to pay into state funds to protect policyholders in case one of the companies should ever fail.

The Legal Reserve System

Every year, all life and annuity insurance companies who are designated as "legal reserve companies" (a requirement in order to do business in most states) must submit annual statements to the insurance departments of each state in which they are licensed. They must give a detailed report of the company's financial status and prove their solvency and compliance with all the insurance laws. A team of State Insurance Department examiners conduct audits so that every *i* is dotted, every *t* is crossed, and every dollar accounted for.

A unique advantage of the legal reserve system is that if one company is purchased by or merged into another, there is no change whatsoever in the policy benefits or premiums. This way, the insurance company has a public responsibility to respect both the letter and the spirit of laws and regulation, so the interests of their policyholders are always protected.

So, in the rare instance of an insurance company's reserve falling short, it goes into what is called "receivership." In the rare instance of that occurring, the remaining insurance companies in the state legal reserve pool must assume the liabilities and obligations of the now-defunct insurer. The amount of the defunct insurer's liability they are required to accept is based on the amount of insurance and annuities the healthy company has issued in that state. If one company has issued 10 percent of all insurance and annuities in that state, then they must accept 10 percent of any bankrupt insurer's obligations for that state.

So, despite the stomach-churning stock plunges, the situation with insurance companies simply doesn't compare with the failed banks. Financial analyst Barry Rabkin of Financial Insights, an IDC company, says of insurance companies: "They're solvent—solidly solvent thanks to conservative investments and tight state regulator oversight." The big companies are "not going anywhere."

He adds that, yes, insurance companies did invest in real estate and mortgages in the years prior to 2008 but not in the huge way the banks did—about 10 percent of investments were in those areas industry-wide. About two-thirds of insurance-company investments are in solid, conservative instruments like federal and municipal bonds. Even AIG, the insurance giant bailed out by the federal government after the crash of 2008, was always solvent in its insurance operation. The losses at AIG came mostly from the unrelated financial-services division, which other insurance companies do not have.

Chapter THIRTEEN

Stages Of Retirement

Money is not a living thing, but it does have one thing in common with all other living things—it is capable of reproducing! Money begets money, which in turn begets more money. It is that one simple attribute of the green stuff, more than any other, which makes comprehensive retirement planning possible.

What is SIPS? It's an acronym for Stages Income Planning System. The basic idea behind SIPS is taking a retirement "nest egg" and strategically splitting it up into smaller sums along a timeline. These sums are then positioned into investment vehicles that are designed to accommodate the special requirements of retirees.

SIPS is not a new concept. Professional income planners have used them for years. It is sometimes referred to as the "bucket" system, or "time buckets." That label is fitting because what we are doing is creating buckets, or accounts of money, that can be used in stages.

Perhaps you were around during the space race years of the 1960s when the United States and the Soviet Union were in a contest to see who could be first to land a man on the moon and bring him home safely. We watched the grainy images on our black-and-white TVs and held our collective breath, as the Saturn V rocket climbed toward outer space. In a somber voice, the announcer intoned, "We have ignition," and with a deafening roar the first stage of the rocket came alive, slowly nudging the thirty-two-story missile upward and away from earth. Glued to the TV, we watched the shaky, glowing image of flame grow smaller and smaller until it was a pinprick of light in the stratosphere. Then we heard the drone of the newscaster tell us, "Stage one has been jettisoned and stage two has taken over."

Our first money stage does the heavy lifting in our retirement since it will be taking care of us during the first ten years of retirement. Meanwhile, other assets are allowed to grow as they wait to fuel our retirement. You and your financial planner will have already identified all the sources of income you can count on during your retirement. Social Security income will figure in, as well as any pensions, IRAs 401(k)s, SEPs, etc. By now, you will have established the answer to the big question: "How much?" How much will it take for me to pay living expenses for my spouse and myself, and still continue to enjoy the independent lifestyle to which we have become accustomed? Because we don't know how long our retirement will last, it is my strong recommendation that we should make sure that the words "guaranteed" and "lifetime" are incorporated into our income-planning strategy. That is what Stage Income Planning Systems do and why I recommend them for many retiring seniors. The final stage of SIPS is designed to accommodate your income needs for life and guarantee that whatever assets remain in your accounts at your death will be passed along to your heirs in the manner in which you intended.

As the first stage finishes and is jettisoned, the second stage kicks in. Now with momentum on its side, it has an easier time pushing its payload into orbit. Similarly, our second money stage provides the same income as the first money stage, but it does so with less of a drain on our total resources. Why? Because we have given it a full ten years to accumulate interest with no withdrawals. Stage two kicks in to give us a guaranteed lifelong income stream, helping us to achieve our retirement orbit so to speak. It is that final boost that provides us with the money we need to successfully retire without altering our lifestyle or worrying about the "what ifs".

So, let's take a look at these money stages, and see how they work.

Getting Started

Let's start with the pre-launch preparations. During the accumulation phase of our life, we will have been acquiring enough money to see us through an emergency. As discussed earlier in this book (where we discussed the three types of money), we call this emergency money. It has been recommended that we have between three- and six-months' worth of income set aside in liquid cash or cash equivalent before we start thinking about retirement.

When I was in school, it was fashionable to wear penny loafers. This is one shoe style that has stood the test of time. They were introduced to the world by a shoemaker by the name of John Bass in 1930 and have shod the feet of such celebrities as President John F. Kennedy and Michael Jackson. But what made them unique was a little slit on the outside of the shoe where a penny could be inserted. But at my school, we were too cool for pennies. We put dimes in the slits of our penny loafers. When I was in the ninth grade, I went to the movies with a pal. We had been dropped off by my parents and were instructed to call them from a pay phone when the movie was over. The only problem was, we had spent every last cent of our money on candy and popcorn. Neither of us had the money to make the call. We were working up the courage to ask the manager to borrow a dime when it dawned on me, "I've got a dime in both of my shoes!" Problem solved.

Like the dimes in my penny loafers, our emergency money has to be readily available. It must be money we can put our hands on when we need it. It is advisable to have it placed in an account where it can be withdrawn by either going up to a teller window, an ATM machine, or writing a check.

Now that we have that out of the way, let's talk about the characteristics of our first money stage of retirement.

Stage One

As mentioned earlier, we need to produce income for ten years at this stage. The money we set aside will depend on how much we need. What safe investment vehicle can we use for money in this stage?

How about certificates of deposit (CDs) at a bank? If we go with this investment vehicle, it would be prudent to stagger, or ladder our CDs. The longer the term of the CD, the more interest it will earn. We will tap into the shortest-term CD first and tap into the longest-term CD last. The net return of these CDs after tax could be higher than treasury bonds. A good place to shop for fixed-interest, laddered maturity investments is a credit union. The interest rates that credit unions offer to their members are usually higher than those offered by banks.

Regardless of what investment you use for this money stage, it is important that your money is safe from loss and that you put enough money in the bucket to get you through the first ten years.

You might also consider an immediate annuity. Many use this strategy because it is hassle-free. Instead of having to physically write yourself a check from your money-market account or go down to the bank as you withdraw from one CD after another, the immediate annuity can be set up to automatically credit your checking account each month. You still maintain control of it, just like any other account, but the annuity is more of a set-it-and-forget-it approach that some retirees prefer.

We have talked about standard fixed annuities and fixed indexed annuities. What is an immediate annuity? By definition, it is a contract issued by an insurance company guaranteeing payments of a specific sum to a retiree each month on a specific date. This can last either for a fixed number of months or for the life of the annuitant (and his or her spouse if you choose).

Some may feel that the definite, regularly scheduled payout provided by immediate annuities is a bit limiting and restrictive. They may not want to live on a budget. If so, then this strategy isn't for them. From an informal poll that I have taken during my listening sessions with retirees, I've found that most of them are fine with living on a budget. But they want to make sure that the budget has enough figured in for travel, entertainment, and recreation. Most say that they feel comfortable and secure with the limitations. Some have felt that if they had all their money available, they might be tempted to spend more than they should.

One retiree related an advantage of using an immediate annuity payout that I hadn't thought of before. "When you want to say 'no' to someone with their hand out, you can always use that old saw 'I'm on a fixed income,'" he said. "You can look them square in the eye and not lie when you tell them that you just don't have it to give." He was quick to add that he could always count on his emergency money if he really needed to lend a helping hand to a loved one.

When listing the pros and cons of using an immediate annuity to fund stage one, it is important to remember that we have the exclusion ratio in our favor. This is the portion of the return on an investment that is income-tax exempt. It represents a payback of initial investments rather than capital gains. Immediate annuities sometimes get a bad rap because once you buy one, you generally can't get your principal back. You have to take the payout all the way to the end. However, this drawback has a bright and shiny silver lining: the tax break they provide. Because an immediate annuity pays out both principal and interest on a fully amortized basis, this dramatically reduces your current income-tax liability. With an immediate annuity, you only pay tax on the pro-rata amount of interest you received in the year you received it. The rest of the interest is deferred until it is withdrawn in the years that follow. Yes, the interest is taxed as ordinary income, but the principal is tax-free because it is a return of your initial investment, assuming it was submitted with after-tax funds.

The long and short of it is this: when you figure in the tax break you get by using an immediate annuity for stage one versus using CDs, you get approximately 30 percent more to spend during your retirement.

So, when placed under the microscope, what are the advantages of using an immediate annuity for stage one?

- It can provide guardrails for the financial highway. It prods you to live within your means. By not having immediate access to your money, you are likely to think twice about expenditures. Don't forget you have your emergency money if you need it.

- The tax advantage of an immediate annuity cannot be over emphasized. You only pay tax on the pro-rata amount of interest you receive in the year you received it. Taxes on the rest are deferred until subsequent years.

- It is safe and dependable. It delivers reliable income on predictable dates.

- It may help avoid unnecessary taxes on Social Security benefits.

- Inheritance is handled outside of probate at death.

So, while not the only choice, there are many advantages to this choice for stage one of our retirement income planning.

Stage Two

When we first watched those brave astronauts ride that rocket into outer space, we couldn't see the jettisoning of stage two. The cameras of those days were just not able to capture an image so many miles high. Then NASA developed the technology to have cameras mounted within the stages themselves to film this process. As stage one burned out and fell to earth, a color-film camera mounted in stage two would capture the burnout and the breakaway. Even today, it is a fascinating sight to behold.

As to where to put our money for this second stage, it's a no-brainer! It seems as if the fixed indexed annuity (FIA) was created for this very purpose. For instance, in one FIA contract the amount of growth guaranteed for the income account is 7.2%. An income rider is required for these types of accounts, but they are extremely attractive for those seeking those two words, "lifetime" and "guarantee," in their financial planning.

Why not use a variable annuity for this money stage? After all, don't they have income riders that can give you an income account that will guarantee you a lifetime income? Yes, some do. But the amount of growth promised by these annuities is usually much lower than those offered by the FIAs. Other disadvantages must also be considered.

Potential Loss Of Capital—Unlike fixed indexed annuities, variable annuities can depreciate in value since your money is actually invested in equities. And not tied to an equity

Management Fees—The entire account incurs a 3–6 percent management fee every year like a mutual fund.

Working with the fixed indexed annuity for stage two will afford us several advantages. We can tack on an income rider that will guarantee a lifetime "pension," as discussed in chapter 10.

By using a product with these features, our retirement-shuttle will be pushed safely into permanent orbit.

A Good Fit, But Not For Everybody

The strategy outlined in this chapter might fit you perfectly. But it might not. You can learn what approach is right for you by meeting with a qualified financial advisor. This brings us to the next section of *Help, I'm Retiring!* With all the businesses out there on the street, how do we go about choosing the right financial advisor?

Chapter FOURTEEN

Are You Prepared For A "Perfect Storm?"

Where were you in the summer of 2000?

That's when the movie "*The Perfect Storm*" hit theatres across the nation. It starred George Clooney as the captain of the *Andrea Gail,* a commercial fishing boat that was lost at sea with no survivors after being caught in a "perfect storm."

The movie and the book (published in 1997 by W.W. Norton and Company) were based on an actual meteorological event that took place in October 1991. First, Hurricane Grace, a category two storm, was moving up from the south. Secondly, a nor'easter which had no name came out of the east and merged with the hurricane. Lastly, an area of low pressure that had developed off the Canadian coast was being pushed southward to join the nor'easter and the hurricane.

The three weather phenomena combined to form a rare meteorological event that weather people call a "perfect storm." It produced 40-foot waves that sank the *Andrea Gail* and tragically claimed the lives of Captain Billy Tyne (played by Clooney in the movie) and his five crew members. The bodies and the fishing vessel were never found.

A "Perfect Storm" In The Financial World Could Kill Your Retirement

Could you experience a financial "perfect storm" that could sink your retirement plan?

Professionals keep an eye out for such dangers. They watch for them just as intently as meteorologists watch for dangerous weather. Personally, from where I watch my "radar", I see three potential problem areas that are a threat:

- National Debt
- Market Bubble
- Human Behavior

Let's talk about each of these.

National Debt - According to CBS News *Money Watch*, in 2000, the United States national debt was a little over five and a half trillion dollars. According to Peter G. Peterson, former U.S. Secretary of Commerce in the Nixon administration, the national debt hit 28 trillion dollars in 2021... *and it is still climbing*!

If you travel to New York City and find your way to the western side of Bryant Park, in the neighborhood of Sixth Avenue between 42nd and 43rd streets, you can see what is called "The National Debt Clock". It is a huge electronic billboard that shows the national debt total ticking up faster than your eyes can register the numbers.

Standing on the sidewalk, looking up at the blizzard of flashing numbers, you may wonder what the danger is. What is the national debt costing us? First of all, the interest on a debt that large is phenomenal. The debt, almost incomprehensible to normal U.S. citizens, is real. One day, the debt will have to be repaid. Think of a credit card with a balance on which you are paying only the interest charges. You are sinking deeper and deeper into debt.

Why is that bad? Every dollar that goes toward the repayment of the debt means a dollar that can't be used to provide goods and services for the future. The debt has not only the potential to impair your financial health, but also that of your children and grandchildren, who will inherit it.

Market Bubble – Are we in a market bubble? As I write this, I think we are. As this book goes to press in the fall of 2021, stocks are generally overpriced. As the term infers, bubbles are illusions. They eventually burst.

According to Macrotrends, a research platform for investors in the stock market, the Dow Jones Industrial Average in 2010 was at 11,577. In 2020 the Dow surged to 30,606. That's a 264 percent increase in 10 years. Are we heading towards bursting that bubble? From my chair, yes, and I'm not the only financial professional who sees it that way. Concern is widespread among my colleagues in the financial advisory profession.

I saw the expressions on the faces of many who lost half their fortunes when the last market bubble burst. They were stunned. It happened suddenly. There was no reaction time. Those losses were real, and it took years for some to recover. Others did not have time to recover. They were forced to spend their resources to keep food on the table and a roof over their heads. Still, others were faced with health crises that syphoned off the resources they had worked so hard to save.

So, if you are a retiree, or nearing retirement, you are the most vulnerable to the bursting of a market bubble. Why? Because you have less time to recover from it.

Human Behavior – What is the time-honored mantra of successful investing? Buy low – Sell high. Right? But, because our emotions are involved, most peoples' investment behavior causes them to follow the markets right to the bottom when they start to tank. Why is that?

One factor is resistance to change. "Hey, the markets always come back!" And that is true – eventually. Time is involved. How much time do you have? Our "come back" period diminishes in length as we age.

Then there is greed. Let's face it – it is human nature to always want more and never be satisfied. This little aspect of human behavior may cause us to hold on to an investment strategy long after the time to change arrives.

Blind optimism. That's when "hope" becomes the strategy. I know many people who are optimists by nature. They see the glass as half full, not half empty. This serves us well in many aspects of life, but not so much when it comes to investing. There is a science to it, and it cannot be wished away. When storm clouds gather, you may *hope* not to get wet. But logic and reason dictate that you reach for an umbrella.

Are You Prepared?

Are you prepared for the "perfect storm" in retirement? When the Andrea Gail left the port of Gloucester, Massachusetts on September 20, 1991, the objective was to head for the Grand Banks of Newfoundland, fill the hold with thousands of pounds of swordfish, put it on ice, and return within a few weeks.

They were successful – until disaster struck. The real reason for the tragedy was that Captain Tyne either didn't know about the weather reports or paid no heed to them.

Instead of putting your trust in your investing instincts, blind luck, or wishful thinking, rely on the science provided by a trained financial professional. Allow a financial advisor (one who is obligated ethically to offer advice *exclusively* in your best interest) to help you prepare for your retirement. If your plan is perfectly tailored to your individual needs and designed to protect you from the financial danger of potential threats, then you will enjoy your sunset years, secure in the knowledge of just where you will be 10, 20 or 30 years from now.

Chapter FIFTEEN

Select The Right Advisor

There are two areas of life in which I would strongly urge you not to procrastinate. One is your health. The other is your wealth.

I was on an airplane recently when an article caught my eye entitled "Ten Reasons Why Men Don't Go to the Doctor." A physician wrote it, and some of the items were humorous. Reason seven was: Going to the doctor is giving in to your nagging wife! The doctor said she had a patient who gave his wife a copy of his prescription for Lipitor as an anniversary gift.

But why is it that some are reluctant to seek the advice of a professional when it comes to their wealth? Could it be that they are confused by the plethora of financial theories and philosophies out there, all of which are put forth by people calling themselves "professionals"?

It is possible to receive conflicting medical advice. I recall that I woke up one morning with severe back pain. My doctor prescribed muscle relaxers. My chiropractor recommended treatment that did not involve medication. I am not a doctor, but it's my back. I took advantage of both opinions, and the pain was gone the next day. Which doctor was right? Perhaps they were both right.

Likewise, when it comes to financial advice, many times there may be two diametrically opposed opinions proffered by two different advisors as to how to grow your money. Both may be legitimately sound and both may work. I say that one should beware of any advisor who closes his/her mind to viable investment alternatives and drives a flag into the ground of an extreme position. Behind the scenes may be the influence of a certain profit motive. If that is what is driving the advice, then where do the advisor's interests lie? Are they with the advisor or with the client?

One advisor may eschew any involvement with the stock market and recommend to his clients that they place all their money in insurance products completely free of market risk. Another advisor may recommend to his clients that "buy and hold" is the answer. Both claim to be professionals. Which one do you believe? Which one can you trust?

I am going to go way out on a limb here and say that neither one is right. In most portfolios, there is a place for stocks, bonds, mutual funds, etc., and there is also a place for safe money alternatives, such as CDs and annuities. If an advisor is polarized in his/her thinking, there is a reason for it; and if it has to do with fees and commissions, then shame on the advisor. It is like a doctor prescribing pills because he/she gets a kickback from the manufacturer.

What To Look For:

1. Certification

Certification means that the advisor has, by obtaining the proper education and training, secured the endorsement of third-party organizations whose job it is to evaluate and designate him or her as being qualified to perform the work that he/she has undertaken. A financial advisor will usually list his/her certification and category of expertise on the business card and on any brochures that include his/her biographical information. These societies of certification, such as Certified Financial Planner and Certified Retirement Financial Advisor and others, require that the advisor receiving the certificate pass rigorous and comprehensive tests covering all matters pertaining to retirement planning. Usually, these tests are administered at a closely monitored testing center by proctors. Once obtained, keeping the certification updated year by year by continuing education and further testing is required. This will assure the client that his advisor is up to date with current tax laws and familiar with industry standards.

2. Experience

My firm, Diversified Estate Solutions, has over forty-five years of experience. My professional designation is CRFA - Certified Retirement Financial Advisor.

The point in telling you this is not to toot my own horn or to plug my practice. But just like a doctor doesn't start his own business without proper training and experience, it would be presumptuous for any financial professional to take on clients without being able to competently guide them with advice based on his training and experience.

3. Is The Advisor A Good Listener?

Being a good listener is the most important quality a financial advisor can have. If this piece isn't present, then all the certifications and designations in the world are just so much business card alphabet soup.

A good financial advisor will refrain from giving advice...until he has listened well enough to know his clients and understands their unique financial situation. Over the years, if I have learned anything about helping people with their problems, it is that every person is unique, and so are his or her tolerances, goals, desires, and dreams. There is no such thing as "one size fits all" in the world of financial counseling. This means that every plan in which a professional design will be like a tailored suit: specifically and specially designed for his unique client. This brings us to our next ingredient to look for in the right financial advisor.

4. Is The Advisor Able To Concentrate On Your Financial Needs?

A competent financial advisor needs to be able to concentrate on preserving your wealth. He should be able to properly guide those who are already retired, as well as point the way for those who are within ten years of retirement. Logically, a financial plan drawn up for someone in his/her thirties and forties would be much different than the one drawn up for someone, say, in his/her sixties or seventies.

In football, many a game is lost because the team doesn't play both halves. I have seen many advisors over the years that are very good during the first half—during the accumulation phase of life—but, for some reason, not the second half, the preservation and income-planning phase. Financial planners and investment advisors generally are familiar with the concepts of diversification and asset allocation. Many advisors, despite a few hiccups here and there, do a pretty good job. But when we start getting those invitations to join AARP, and we begin to qualify for those senior discounts on coffee at McDonalds, our thinking changes when it comes to our money too. There is a window, if you will, of five to ten years on either side of retirement. And typically, those who are in that window change their mode of thinking from one of accumulation to one of preservation and income planning. A good advisor will be sensitive to this. This is the second half of the game, so to speak. Blow this call, and it's game over for a retiree. So, when choosing an advisor, look for one that has that sensitivity that enables him/her to customize advice for retirement. A good financial advisor will find out what the risk tolerance of his client is. This can be discerned only by asking questions and listening to the answers. With few exceptions, as we age, our risk tolerance is less.

5. Does The Advisor Understand And Address Taxation?

I once saw a bumper sticker that read: "It's not how much you make, it's how much you get to keep that matters." One commonality we all have is taxes. When you are choosing an advisor, look for one who understands how taxes work and what impact they can have on us, especially during retirement.

This is one area that is often missed by financial advisors, especially when it comes to individual retirement accounts. A competent advisor will take the time to educate his client on the strategies available to him so as to prevent Uncle Sam from being the IRA's biggest beneficiary. He will ask to see the IRA document and pay particular attention to the designated beneficiary form, since it is so critically important in making sure that the client's money, if not used up in retirement, goes to heirs in the manner in which he intended.

6. Does The Advisor Understand And Address Insurance?

A good advisor will not try to just sell insurance to his client. He/she will explain the value that insurance can have to the clients, especially those who are retiring. He will know how insurance works and be able to offer clients advice on what options are available. The advisor will want to make sure that the clients are neither underinsured nor over insured and will be sensitive to their preferences in this regard. In the last few years, many sophisticated strategies have been devised by competent advisors using insurance to enable their clients to "have their cake and eat it too." Early in the book we wrote about the taxation problems of an IRA. Let's say that you don't think you will need your IRA for income during retirement. Why not pass as much of it as possible on to your heirs by using a strategy involving life insurance? That way you will be able to provide money to them tax-free. One client who had turned seventy years and six months was dismayed to find that he was forced to take something called "required minimum distributions" from his IRA. (Age before the SECURE Act was implemented). He didn't need the money. He didn't want the money. The light bulb went off for him when he learned that he could take the RMDs (which he had to take anyway) and use it to buy life insurance. Now, when he dies, instead of passing that money to his heirs in a taxable form, it will be, because of the rules of life insurance, tax-free! In fact, when we crunched the numbers, assuming he lived another ten years, his legacy would be more than double what his IRA would have been worth. Some life-insurance companies may provide long-term coverage at no extra charge. A competent advisor will know how to implement this strategy.

7. Does The Advisor Understand And Address Estate Planning?

The competent advisor will give attention to proper estate planning. It is likely that, without this detail being cared for, our heirs will pay much more in taxes than they should. There is something out there called the "estate tax," or as some like to call it, the "death tax." It is a moving target. Congress can change the estate-tax exemption at will, it seems, so we won't really know whether we will be affected by this tax until the time comes. But a good advisor will always be on top of this. The advisor will have a current understanding of taxes. He/she will also be able to tell us what to look for in arranging our affairs so as to avoid paying this tax if possible, using perfectly legitimate provisions made by the IRS for our benefit. You might say that, when it comes to taxes, he/she will have the map to the minefield and be able to guide clients safely through it. The advisor will have a grasp of what function wills and trusts play in a properly structured retirement and be able to provide resources to his client to properly facilitate these legal documents as needed.

Historical and Future Federal Estate Tax Exemptions and Rates

Year	Estate Tax Exemption	Top Estate Tax Rate
1997	$600,000	55%
1998	$625,000	55%
1999	$650,000	55%
2000	$675,000	55%
2001	$675,000	55%
2002	$1,000,000	50%
2003	$1,000,000	49%
2004	$1,500,000	48%
2005	$1,500,000	47%
2006	$2,000,000	46%
2007	$2,000,000	45%
2008	$2,000,000	45%
2009	$3,500,000	45%
2010	Repealed	Repealed
2011	$5,000,000	35%
2012	$5,120,000	35%
2013	$5.250,000	40%
2014	$5,340,000	40%
2015	$5,430,000	40%
2016	$5,450,000	40%
2017	$5,490,000	40%
2018	$11,180,000	40%
2019	$11,400,000	40%
2020	$11,580,000	40%
2021	$11,058,000	40%

Is The Advisor Independent And Universal In Approach?

A good financial-advisory firm will be independent. This will ensure that no conflict of interest exists that could prevent an unbiased and open-handed financial plan. The financial advisor you choose to work with should have an entire universe of solutions at his/her disposal that the advisor can, in turn, recommend to clients if they fit.

8. Does The Advisor Treat All Clients In A Fiduciary Manner?

Make sure your advisor or someone on his team is a fiduciary. Fee-based-only advisors will be driven, not by commissions, but solely by the needs of the client. This removes the possibility of clients having to absorb unwarranted hidden fees, whether they show up on the front end or on the back of transactions made or contracts implemented.

The right financial advisory firm will also have the capability of being both a money manager to handle stocks, bonds, mutual funds, equity traded funds, REITS, etc., and be able to serve a qualified advisor for investment vehicles provided by such institutions as banks and insurance companies, like CDs and annuities.

As one advisor recently stated at a conference on fiduciary representation, "Having no secrets keeps us all on the same side of the table, and I like that." Ditto to that.

If a fixed account from a bank or insurance strategy makes sense, then we charge no fee because we get a fee from them. We find that most advisors are either insurance agents or independent investment advisors.

The Right Advisor

Independent Insurance Agency	Independent Investment Advisors
Life Insurance	Stocks
Long Term Care Coverage	Bonds
Fixed Annuities	Mutual Funds
Indexed Annuities	Exchange-Traded Funds
Certificate of Deposits (CDs)	Real Estate Investment Trusts
Medicare Supplements	Variable Annuities
	Fee Only Money Management
No Fee at all	*Fee only, No commissions to team*

Pros and Cons

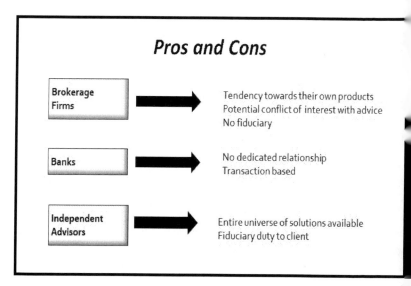

Brokerage Firms → Tendency towards their own products
Potential conflict of interest with advice
No fiduciary

Banks → No dedicated relationship
Transaction based

Independent Advisors → Entire universe of solutions available
Fiduciary duty to client

Influences

When a colleague of mine, Matt Zagula, first introduced me to his friend Rocky Bleier, I was immediately impressed. The famous former NFL running back possessed, not one, but four diamond-studded Super-Bowl rings, which he was gracious enough to allow me to wear when I posed for a photograph with him.

The first thing I noticed about this outstanding man is that he is of ordinary physical stature. I was surprised when I stood next to him to see that he was about my size, in fact, five foot eleven. But, as I would soon learn, he has a heart as big as all outdoors. After his 1968 rookie season with the Pittsburgh Steelers, Bleier was drafted into the army and volunteered for duty in Vietnam. While on patrol, he was wounded in the left thigh by a rifle bullet when his platoon was ambushed in a rice paddy. Then, an enemy grenade exploded nearby sending shrapnel into his lower right leg. He was awarded both the Purple Heart and the Bronze Star. Doctors told him that his football career was over and that he would do well just to walk without limping

But one year after being wounded, Bleier reported to the Steelers' training camp. He was down to 180 pounds and couldn't walk without pain. He spent two years working out, just trying to gain a spot on the active roster. Finally, in the summer of 1974 he was in the Steelers' starting lineup.

"I just never gave up," he told the crowd. "The reason I worked so hard was so that, at some time in the future, I wouldn't have to ask myself, 'What if?'"

My mother, Cathy Parkes, was a pert and active ninety-five-year-old who stood five foot five inches tall and weighed about 76 pounds. She was a dynamic woman. She always wore a smile, regardless of what unpleasantness came her way. I am convinced that it is her angelically cheerful disposition that kept her going so strong. Although a diminutive nonagenarian, she loved doing things for others and had quite a reputation for it among those who knew her.

Cathy Parkes drummed into her three sons those principles of cheerfulness and unselfishness, and I have nothing but gratitude for her sometimes strict, but loving upbringing. She was fond of often repeating the golden rule, her version of which was: "Do as you would be done by," which, I suppose, is a shorter version of "Do unto others as you would have them do unto you." With her, honesty was not just a virtue, and a character quality to be aimed at; it was a nonnegotiable requirement to be part of the family. That is the reason why, I suppose, that even now, when I am giving financial advice to my clients, I speak to them as if I were speaking to my own mother, father, brother, or sister.

If Rocky Bleier suffered any pain from his war wounds, he hid it well. His broad smile was infectious and became even more radiant when he was discussing his years on the gridiron. As he slipped the four Super Bowl rings off his fingers and I placed them onto mine for the photograph, I noticed that one of the rings was stamped "Super Bowl IX 1975." It occurred to me that about the same time Rocky was dodging Viking defensive players on his way to helping the Steelers beat Fran Tarkenton and company 16–6, I was about to enter the world of financial planning.

My career began as an agent behind a desk in a Durham County, North Carolina, office of Farm Bureau Insurance Company in 1976. It was property and casualty insurance, insuring homes and cars against fires and accidents. My wife, Dianne, and I were a young couple, and it paid the bills. But it was not exciting work.

Thanks to my mother, I had developed the habit of being a good listener, and I began to see that there were many opportunities to help those who sat across the desk from me other than simply providing them with liability and collision insurance. It came natural to me to want to use the tools at my disposal as a means of solving problems for people. I began to explore the world of future planning for my clients in a new light. I was intrigued when I discovered that one could use annuities to protect assets in retirement, and that there was more to life insurance than a check to the widow at her husband's death. Newer strategies were becoming available.

I noticed during my client interviews that most people were grateful when I took the time to pull back the curtain and explain both sides of making a decision when it came to their finances. I discovered that nobody wanted to be *sold*, but everyone appreciated being *told*. My "book of business" at the agency drew the attention of the agency manager because it was lopsided compared to the norm. Many of my clients were enrolled in programs that had to do with managing their entire financial lives, not just insuring their cars and homes. I was not even conscious of this until the manager took me aside and pointed it out. He told me that he had been in his position for more than thirty years, and then he very unselfishly suggested that perhaps I should pursue a career as an independent financial advisor. I am very grateful to him for that little piece of advice. I may sound corny, but when I was at that agency, I actually viewed those people on the other side of my desk as friends. I felt like it was my job to help them solve their problems if I could. That is still a mantra I endorse and for which I offer no apologies. By the way, I followed my manager's advice, and have never regretted the decision.

I know that eventually I will come to the retirement crossroads myself. And perhaps I will slow down, but I can't see taking down the sign and hanging up the spurs entirely as long as I am physically able to lend a helping hand to others who have problems concerning their finances. I simply enjoy it that much. To me, nothing is as rewarding in the business world as going home at night knowing that I have in some way improved the lives of others through the expertise and skill that I have garnered over the years.

Not too long ago, a sixty-two-year-old woman entered my office and seemed very upset. She had just been relieved from her place of employment after having worked there for more than thirty years. She dabbed at her eyes as she told her story. Apparently, she had been given her notice of termination rather coldly and within months of when she would have been eligible to receive her pension. As it was, she was worried about where she could find another job to make ends meet.

As I listened, it did seem that her situation was dire, that is until she told me that she had a 401(k) that was worth almost $300,000. She did not realize the power of her savings and the effect compound interest could have on her nest egg. She also did not know anything about the income-planning strategies that had become available in the past few years.

When she learned that her Social Security payments, in addition to a small alimony check, combined with the lifetime income arrangement we were able to hammer out of her IRA, would be enough for her to start her retirement right then, her tears showed up again...but this time they were tears of joy.

I'm sure it's the feeling doctors get when they are able to tell a patient that the operation was a success, and that they will not be confined to a wheelchair after all!

Another thing that affected my decision to choose the career I did was watching my seven-year-old daughter Shannon struggle with, and finally, after two years, succumb to leukemia. My wife and I went through a variety of emotions over time. Memories that were made in our love for her—no one can take them away from us. That experience, while painful, taught me many things. It taught me that, as the wise King Solomon wrote in the holy scriptures, "Time and unforeseen occurrence befall us all." Shannon's illness was sudden and completely unexpected. It was definitely an unforeseen occurrence for our family. I realized that if such a thing could befall a family such as ours and affect us in the deepest way, then it could happen to any family. It certainly gave new meaning to my role as a planner for people. My career took on a new importance with the knowledge that no one knows what the future may hold and that being prepared for contingencies is not just a slogan on a billboard or a sound bite of a commercial. I had a very important job to do. Some things are beyond our control, of course. But we should strive to control the things we can.

During the heady days of the 1990s when money placed in the stock market could do nothing but multiply, I remember the talking heads on television making the wide-eyed prediction that it would never end. Many well-educated market analysts said that this Wall Street gold rush was good for at least another few decades and that we were within sight of utopia. There were many of us who wanted to believe it, but deep inside just knew better.

The downturn began in September of 2000 and was soon in a free fall. The NASDAQ, the darling of the dot coms, fell 78.4 percent from its high of 5,132 in March of 2000 to a sickening 1,108 by October of the same year. The crash of 2000 resulted in a loss of almost $8 trillion in wealth, a figure that is hard to wrap the mind around.

Those of us who had been around for some time in the financial industry were not surprised to see it happen. Bear markets are cyclical beasts, coming back, on average, every four years or so. The appearance of this bear was overdue! We had enjoyed a great run for nearly two decades. The correction had to happen.

I remember talking to people in the 1990s about taking a part of their portfolio and moving it to a position where it could be guaranteed safe against market losses.

"Why would I want to do that?" asked one man. "Everything is going up. I just need to invest more in the market."

Seeing so many lose so much wealth so quickly impressed upon me the importance of staying with the tried-and-true disciplines of managing money. There are two phases of our economic lives—the accumulation phase, which starts in our twenties and continues into our fifties or sixties, and the preservation-distribution phase, which carries us through our retirement years.

Looking back, I am glad that there were families whose wealth I was able to help preserve during those turbulent years. As a result of Comprehensive Financial Planning, many of my clients successfully dodged that calamity and went on to have fulfilling retirement years as a result.

For the most part, the stock market subsequently recovered from the 2000 crash and fortunately, some were wiser than before. When the housing bubble and the credit crisis caused the next market correction from 2007 to 2009, fewer lost their fortunes. Again, I am thankful to have been able to pass along the principles of Comprehensive Retirement Planning that helped save some of that wealth for retirees just when they needed it the most.

Sleep Well At Night

Years ago, a farmer owned land along the Atlantic seacoast and advertised for hired hands. There were few applicants. Many were reluctant to work on farms along the coast because of the frequent storms that could wreak havoc on the buildings and crops. Just when the farmer thought he wouldn't be able to hire anyone for the job, a short, thin man, well past middle age, approached him and asked about the position.

"What makes you a good farm hand?" the farmer asked him.
"I can sleep on a stormy night," the man answered.

Although puzzled by this answer, the farmer, desperate for help, hired him. The little man worked well around the farm, busy from dawn to dusk, and the farmer felt satisfied with the man's work. Then one night the wind howled loudly from an offshore storm. Jumping out of bed, the farmer grabbed a lantern and rushed next door to the hired hand's sleeping quarters. He shook the new man and yelled "get up. A storm is coming! Tie things down before they blow away." The little man rolled over in bed and said firmly, "No, sir. I told you I can sleep through a stormy night."

Enraged by the response, the farmer was tempted to fire him on the spot. Instead, he hurried outside to prepare for the storm. To his amazement, he discovered that all of the haystacks had been covered with tarpaulins. The cows were in the barn, the chickens were in the coops, and the doors were barred. The shutters were tightly secured. Everything was tied down. Nothing could blow away. The farmer then understood what his hired hand had meant, so he returned to his own bed to sleep while the wind blew.

The hired hand in the story was able to sleep because he had secured against the storm. He had anticipated uncertainty and had prepared for it.

We hope for the best. We plan for the worst. We **Sleep Well At Night.**

About The Author

Rick Parkes, CRFA (Certified Retirement Financial Advisor) has been practicing since 1976. The CRFA is a financial-advisor certification program that he has completed, and which provides high impact, up-to-date courses on a wide range of services and products. This enables him to continuously expand his knowledge and explore new markets in keeping with changing strategies that he helps implement to meet the client's financial goals.

Issues covered on CRFA continuing education.

- New research on financial issues that impact retirees
- Tax changes that affect retirees
- Use of life insurance in a qualified plan
- Use of an irrevocable trust with the grantor's right to invade principal

How vital is CRFA™ designation if the CPA or CFP® is already there?

- CPA brands the advisor as a "tax specialist" in the mind of the layperson.
- CFP® brands the advisor as a financial planning generalist.
- Certified Retirement Financial Advisor™ brands the advisor as a specialist in retiree financial issues.

The instruction and continuing education required by these programs contain dense content that meets rigorous industry standards as follows:

- Three years of experience in financial services now mandatory to gain CRFA™ designation
- Proctored exam
- Exam pass rate on first try at 70 percent
- Ethics CE required annually

Rick has been seen or published in the following media:

- MONEY magazine
- FORBES magazine
- Business Journal
- New York Times
- Chicago Tribune
- Chicago Sun Times
- USA Today
- Entrepreneur Magazine
- Yahoo Finance
- Morningstar
- Market Watch
- Reuters
- Business Week
- Wall Street Journal
- Newsweek

- Thestreet.com
- CNBC
- NBC
- ABC
- Fox
- CBS

Rick is also widely known as a radio talk-show host entitled "Retirement Income Show", in which he discusses financial matters of importance to his listeners, such as income planning for their retirement and protecting their assets in a volatile and unpredictable market.

Parkes Principles

Retirement Wisdom Collected From Throughout The World

"I not only use all the brains that I have, but all I can borrow." - *Woodrow Wilson*

When I first saw this quote by Woodrow Wilson, I realized that I had something in common with the 28th president. I may not always know it, but if I know someone who does that's almost as good.

Wilson was noted for his intelligence. He was a professor at Princeton University and became its president in 1910. He went to law school at the University of Virginia and practiced in Atlanta, Georgia. In 1883 he entered John Hopkins University where he did graduate work in political science and history. His doctoral dissertation in 1885 brought academic appointments from Bryn Mawr College and Wesleyan University. Wilson remains the most academically qualified president, being the only one thus far to receive a doctorate. I could go on, but suffice it to say
the guy was pretty smart. But do you know what the greatest single sign of his intelligence was? He knew how much he did not know. He loved consensus, sought to build it in all his endeavors, especially when he served as the President of the United States. He was known for seeking and obtaining knowledge from anyone who could bring it to the table. I love the quote. Do that and you will keep learning. Do that with your finances and your wealth will grow.

Parkes
Principles

Retirement Wisdom Collected From Throughout
The World

Benjamin Franklin's Advice About Money

Here is something written by Benjamin Franklin that
relates to money management. If more people followed
this strategy, they would not have a problem with their
finances in their retirement.

"When I was a child of seven years old, my friends, on a
holiday, filled my pocket with halfpence. I went directly
to a shop where they sold toys for children; and, being
charmed with the sound of a whistle, that I met by the
way in the hands of another boy, I voluntarily offered
and gave all my money for it. When I came home,
whistling all over the house, much pleased with my
whistle, but disturbing all the family, my brothers,
sisters, and cousins, understanding the bargain I had
made, told me I had given four times as much for it as it
was worth; put me in mind what good things I might
have bought with the rest of the money; and laughed at
me so much for my folly, that I cried with vexation; and
the reflection gave me more chagrin than the whistle
gave me pleasure. This, however, was afterwards of use
to me, the impression continuing on my mind; so that
often, when I was tempted to buy some unnecessary
thing, I said to myself, do not give too much for the
whistle; and I saved my money."

BENJAMIN FRANKLIN, letter to Madame Brillon,
November10, 1779. - The Works of
Benjamin Franklin, ed. Jared Sparks, vol. 2, p. 181
(1836)

I don't think Ben would mind if we substituted "car" or "house" or "vacation" for the "whistle".

Parkes
Principles

Retirement Wisdom Collected From Throughout
The World

***"Anyone who stops learning is old, whether
at twenty or eighty. Anyone who keeps
learning stays young."*** - *Henry Ford*

Up until his death at age 83 in 1947, Henry Ford, the
father of American mass production, could often be
found in the ford engineering laboratory, tinkering, and
discovering. Studies have shown that our mental
facilities are best protected when we use them. Older
folk who carries on learning and who stay mentally
active are much less likely to suffer from an illness like
Alzheimer's disease.

Ford's career was one of the most astonishing in
industrial history. When he was 40, his friends thought
he was a failure. Just a day-dreaming mechanic who
would rather tinker with odd machines than work at a
steady job. But in a dozen years he was internationally
famous,
and his Model T automobile was changing American life.
When he was 13, he took a watch apart and put it back
together again. He had to do this secretly at night, after
chores on the farm, because his father wanted to
discourage his mechanical ambitions.

Learn something new and grow younger each day.

Parkes Principles

Retirement Wisdom Collected From Throughout The World

"Surplus wealth is a sacred trust which its possessor is bound to administer in his lifetime for the good of the community."
- *Andrew Carnegie*

Can you imagine becoming the richest person in the world and then giving your money away? That's exactly what Andrew Carnegie did. One of the captains of industry of 19th century America, Andrew Carnegie helped build the formidable American steel industry, a process that turned a poor young man into one of the richest entrepreneurs of his age. When he sold his company for $480 million to J.P. Morgan, he retired at the age of 66 as the world's richest man and began his new occupation as philanthropist. His new job was to systematically give his collected fortune away to cultural, educational and scientific institutions for "the improvement
of mankind."

He was fond of saying that "the man who dies rich dies disgraced," Carnegie then turned his attention to giving away his fortune. He abhorred charity, and instead put his money to use helping others help themselves. By the time his life was over, he gave away 350 million dollars. What a legacy!

Parkes
Principles

Retirement Wisdom Collected From Throughout
The World

"It is futile to try to predict the economy and interest rates." - *Peter Lynch*

Peter Lynch managed the fidelity Magellan fund from
1977 to 1990, during which time the fund's assets grew
from $20 million to $14 billion. Often described as a
"chameleon," Peter Lynch adapted to whatever
investment style worked at the time. It is said that his
work
schedule, the equivalent of what we would call today
"24/7," did not have a beginning and an end. He talked
to company executives, investment managers, industry
experts and analysts around the clock.

Apart from this punishing work ethic, Lynch did
consistently apply a set of eight fundamental principles
to his stock selection process:

• Know what you own.

• It's futile to predict the economy and interest
rates.

• You have plenty of time to identify exceptional
companies.

• Avoid long shots.

• Good management is very important - buy good
businesses.

- Be flexible, and humble, and learn from mistakes.

- Before you make a purchase, you should be able to explain why you're buying.

- There's always something to worry about.

Parkes Principles

Retirement Wisdom Collected From Throughout The World

"Sometimes your best investments are the ones you don't make." - *Donald Trump*

Whether you like him or not, Donald Trump has been successful when it comes to money management and investing. This flamboyant television personality, real estate magnate and our 45th President of the United States has a world-wide reputation for savvy business dealings.

Trump is the one who advised others to always "listen to your gut, no matter how good something sounds on paper." He also said, "You are generally better off sticking with what you know." I agree with both accounts. The recession of 1989 caused him to declare business bankruptcy and left him on the brink of personal bankruptcy. Lesson learned that one can bite off more than one can chew, he plowed back into the same arena in which his family had made its fortune - real estate -and climbed out of personal debt, paying off over $900 million.

By the late nineties he was whole again and again was a household name associated with wealth. In 2016, he was elected as our 45th President in the largest Electoral College landslide for a Republican in 28 years.

"The Donald", who is an early baby boomer (born in 1946) is a model of what not to do and then what to do once you've done it. No one has better credentials with which to make the above observation.

Parkes
Principles

Retirement Wisdom Collected From Throughout
The World

"Being the richest man in the cemetery doesn't matter to me. Going to bed at night saying we've done something wonderful... that's what matters to me." - *Steve Jobs*

When Steve Jobs, founder of Apple, died in 2011, many people who worked for Apple, the company he founded in his early twenties, wept openly. This was a mute testimony to the impact he left on the computer world and the world in general. When Jobs was 23 years old, he was worth over one million dollars. When he was 24, he was worth over ten million dollars. A year later at age 25, he was worth over $250,000 million. He said it wasn't that important because "I never did it for the money." When you read what is written about him and hear recordings of his speeches, you believe him.

"Almost everything – all external expectations, all pride, all fear of embarrassment or failure – these things just fall away in the face of death, leaving only what is truly important. Remembering that you are going to die is the best way I know to avoid the trap of thinking you have something to lose. You are already naked. There is no reason not to follow your heart."

Steve Jobs' Stanford Commencement Address.

Parkes
Principles

Retirement Wisdom Collected From
Throughout The World

"The human mind is incredible...."
- Mary Kay Ash

You may remember Mary Kay Ash from the huge
cosmetics company she built and perhaps from the
trademark pink Cadillacs she used to present as
awards to her top
salespeople, however, I remember her more for some of
her axioms such as the following:

*"The human mind is incredible. And, for that
matter, so are the minds of all living creatures.
God programmed a tiny spider, for instance, to
weave a web. He programmed a salmon to swim
thousands of miles upstream to the exact location
where it was hatched. If the brains of spiders and
salmon can be programmed to perform such feats,
imagine what capability of the human brain can
achieve."*

*"It's not so much what happened to us as how we
react to what happens that makes the difference.
Cultivate the happy side of life. Have you ever
stopped to think about how, when something really
bad happens to us, we later see that it really
happened to the best? That's so often true. So, look
for the silver lining in that cloud. It is there."*

*"When children know their mothers believe in
them, they develop self-confidence. On the other*

hand, if a parent repeatedly tells a child that he's shy, he's stupid, he's mean or he's going to grow up to be a bank robber, he'll probably develop that quality or bring that vision to pass."

Parkes
Principles

Retirement Wisdom Collected From Throughout
The World

"If you see a snake, just kill it - don't appoint a committee on snakes."
- *Ross Perot*

Ross Perot was a salesman for IBM when he founded
Electronic Data Systems in 1962. Perot managed to turn
EDS into a multi-billion-dollar corporation, becoming
one of America's richest men. Most people remember
Perot as the short fellow with the big ears who was a
surprise candidate for president in 1992. But don't let
his stature fool you. He is a scrapper. In 1979, tired
of the government's inaction, Ross Perot launched his
own private mission to Iran to rescue two hostages who
were employees of his company.

His straight talking, folksy manner strikes a chord with
me. I share his disdain for red tape and his desire to get
things done. The story goes that when Perot sold EDS to
General Motors for $2.55 billion, he envisioned being
able to stay on as a consultant and actually have an
impact on the giant automaker's culture since now he
technically worked for them. But his scrappy nature
collided with the GM bureaucracy almost immediately.

At one point he said, "I had several memorable
experiences with the GM. It just drove me crazy that
when a customer had a problem with a defective engine,
we wanted to treat it as a class action suit rather than
fix the engine."

Parkes
Principles

Retirement Wisdom Collected From Throughout
The World

*"I believe that if you show people the
problems and you show them the solutions
they will be moved to act."* - *Bill Gates*

I am partial to this slice of wisdom from Microsoft
founder Bill Gates because it's so true. Most of us just
want our problems solved. We just want the answer and
we don't need to hear the sales pitch. We also don't need
to be nagged into action. If given the right information
and the proper tools, we know what to do. The
commercials that irritate me the most on television are
the ones that come at you like a freight train, yelling for
your attention. Is it just me, or are just about all
automobile dealership commercials annoying? Gates'
approach is low key. If his solution to a problem is a
good one, acting on it will be a "no brainer". No need to
dress up in a clown suit and yell. Much of his early work
developing the computer operating system that
now spans the globe was simply solving the problem of
how to effectively type a letter or make a list or create a
spreadsheet. The rest is just so many details.

Gates is noted for having his "think weeks". Twice a
year, he goes to a quiet place with no distractions just to
read suggestions from Microsoft idea people and just
think. Next time you have a problem to work out you
might want to try your own version of "think week" or, if
you're anything like me, a "think day" would do nicely.

Parkes
Principles

Retirement Wisdom Collected From Throughout
The World

*"The time to repair the roof is when the sun
is shining."* - *John F. Kennedy*

There are two kinds of people in this world... those who
practice prevention and those who manage by
emergency. Prevention is so much better when it comes
to maintaining our health. How foolish it would be to
wait until we contract some ailment as a consequence of
our neglect. Likewise, when it comes to our wealth,
doing some planning when retirement is still some
distance ahead of us instead of waiting until it is at our
doorstep is just the sensible and responsible thing to do.

In speaking at engagements, I will sometimes tell of a
friend who feared doctors and resisted getting checkups.
When he did go to see the doctor, it was usually because
of a pain. He always hoped the pain was something
minor and that a prescription of pills could make it
disappear. Usually that was the case, too. So, managing
health by emergency became a pattern for him.
That is, until one visit when the doc informed him that
he had an unstoppable cancer that would end his life
within a year. The sad thing is that the cancer could
have been prevented with a yearly checkup.

Those who fail to plan, plan to fail. It's just that simple.

Parkes Principles

Retirement Wisdom Collected From Throughout The World

"Be thankful for what you have; you'll end up having more. If you concentrate on what you don't have, you will never, ever have enough." - *Oprah Winfrey*

According to some assessments, Oprah Winfrey is the most influential person in the world. Born in 1954 on a hardscrabble Mississippi farm, she rose to become a world-renowned talk show host and one of the richest women in the world.

Winfrey landed a job in radio while still in high school and began co-anchoring the local evening news at the age of 19. Her emotional ad-lib delivery eventually got her transferred to the daytime-talk-show arena and the rest is history.

What makes the above quotation so interesting is that it comes from her. Winfrey is believed to be one of the richest African American women of the 21st century, worth well over three billion dollars. Forbes' international rich list has Oprah as the first African American woman billionaire in world history.

Parkes
Principles

Retirement Wisdom Collected From Throughout
The World

**"It's only when the tide goes out that you
learn who's been swimming naked."**
-   *Warren Buffett*

A perfect example of the above statement is Enron. You
remember, the company whose name will live in infamy
because of the assorted frauds, embezzlements and
accounting practices that were uncovered, all of which
eventually led to its collapse.

The human disaster that resulted from the fall of Enron
far outweighed the corporate disaster, however.
Approximately 11,000 employees had 401(k) funds
invested exclusively in Enron stock and were forbidden
by Enron's own rules from diversifying. They were left
hanging out to dry, their hopes of a comfortable
retirement dashed against the rocks.

World Com, the cell phone company, is another example
of this quote in action. While these stocks were flying
high, no one had a clue that there was a problem. Only
when the "tide" went out, share prices fell, and what was
once covered up was revealed for the world to see. Did
the world see clearly that somebody had been skinny-
dipping in the pond? By then, however, it was too late
for many.

Parkes
Principles

Retirement Wisdom Collected From Throughout
The World

Great Estate Planning Mistakes Made By Celebrities

Celebrities lead different lives when it comes to their
estates. They have different challenges than the rest of
us. They often die leaving great wealth, personal brands
worth millions that survive long after their demise and
intellectual property, such as songs, movies, and even
their images that generate royalties long after death.
Because they are immortalized by their fame, they
sometimes think they are personally immortal too, and
fail to plan for the unexpected until it is too late.

Elvis Presley

Elvis Presley died of a drug overdose in Memphis,
Tennessee on August 16, 1977, at the age of 42. He was
rich and famous, and this is probably the most
notorious example of a poorly planned estate.

His mistake was this: About 73 percent of his 10-
million-dollar estate was lost in the probate process and
to estate taxes and other settlement costs. This left his
heirs with less than $3 million. Had Elvis had a trust,
this could have been avoided. A revocable living trust
can be used to avoid the costs and delays associated
with the probate process.   In most states this type of
trust even keeps the disposition of the estate out of
public view. The estate plan must also focus on
minimizing estate taxes. Of course, Elvis did get the last
laugh because ironically as things turned out, the King

of Rock and Roll earned more money after he died than he ever did while he was alive.

Marilyn Monroe

When Marilyn Monroe died in 1962, she left the rights to her licensing and royalty deals to her acting coach, Lee Strasberg. Today, those royalties generate millions of dollars a year. The odd thing is that they're enriching a woman that Monroe never met, as Strasberg left them to his widow in 1982.

Most recently, a federal court found that Marilyn Monroe was a New Yorker when she died, which means that her estate, Marilyn Monroe LLC, which has earned more than 30 million dollars licensing her image, cannot control the licensing. Product makers may be free to use her image without paying licensing fees to her estate because of a difference between California and New York state laws.

James Brown

If James Brown, the Godfather of Soul, could see the way his estate is unraveling, he wouldn't be saying, "I feel good." He would probably be lamenting. The problems began when his wife since 2001, Tomi Rae Hynie, and their purported 6-year-old son, James Joseph Brown II, were locked out of their Beach Island, SC mansion with eight padlocks, courtesy of some of Brown's children from previous relationships. Funeral arrangements were the next problem. At issue was where the entertainer was to be buried. His older children and most recent wife couldn't agree. After three months, he was finally laid to rest in Augusta, Georgia.

Brown had drafted a will in August 2000 and subsequently an irrevocable trust into which all rights to his music and to the 60-acre Beach Island mansion were placed. Then he had two major life events take place: James II was born 10 months later, and in December of 2001, he and Ms. Hynie were married without a prenuptial agreement. The 15-year legal battle was finally brought to a close after the family reached a settlement over the late singer's estate.

Legal fees consumed huge chunks of the reported $100 million to $200 million he left behind and an eventual gigantic federal estate tax bill will be due.

Michael Jackson

Michael Jackson did a few things right. He chose executors outside the family to manage many of the affairs of his estate. But where he may have erred was by choosing his aging mother to serve as the guardian of his young children with Diana Ross as a backup (entertainer and former member of the Supremes). What happens if his mother dies before his youngest child is an adult? Would the children uproot their lives to live with Ross?

Jimi Hendrix

When Jimi Hendrix, one of the greatest guitarists in musical history, died suddenly in 1970, his legend and his music lived on. The problem was, he left no will. It took almost three decades of litigation before Jimi's father, Al Hendrix, regained control of his son's recordings. When Al died in 2002, he left most of the estate to his adopted daughter, Janie, and left his younger son, Leon Morris Hendrix, out of the will altogether.

Leon and Jimi grew up together in Seattle and remained close. When their father died, Leon sued to get a piece of the estate, and lost. As it turns out, Jimi's blood relatives are left with nothing. And Janie, the stepsister, controls the estate, which still successfully markets Jimi's music.

Conclusion

The list goes on, but the principle is this: If your estate is substantial enough that it could or should last more than one generation, and if you agree with Warren Buffett, who said that he wants to leave his children "enough money so that they would feel that they could do anything, but not so much that they could do nothing," then you need to carefully consider how to set up your estate to make sure your money gets to the people you intend it to go to.

Made in the USA
Columbia, SC
26 October 2022

70032043R00078